BECOMING A TRIBE OF HEARTS

photo by W. Michael (Wolfie) Dooley

About the Author

Raven Kaldera is a polyamorous Pagan activist, northern-tradition shaman, astrologer, prolific author, and storyteller. He lives with his wife, boyfriend, and extended poly Pagan family on a homestead in Massachusetts.

'Tis an ill wind that blows no minds.

PAGAN
POLYAMORY

BECOMING A TRIBE OF HEARTS

RAVEN
KALDERA

Llewellyn Publications
Woodbury, Minnesota

FIRST EDITION
First Printing, 2005

Book design and editing by Rebecca Zins
Cover design and heart image by Gavin Dayton Duffy

Llewellyn is a registered trademark of Llewellyn Worldwide, Ltd.

Library of Congress Cataloging-in-Publication Data
Kaldera, Raven
     Pagan polyamory: becoming a tribe of hearts / Raven Kaldera. —1st ed.
       p. cm.
     ISBN-13: 978-0-7387-0762-4
     ISBN-10: 0-7387-0762-7
     1. Non-monogamous relationships. 2. Sexual ethics. 3. Intimacy (Psychology). 4. Love.
  I. Title.

HQ980.K35 2005
308.84'23—dc22

2005051034

Llewellyn Worldwide does not participate in, endorse, or have any authority or responsibility concerning private business transactions between our authors and the public.

    All mail addressed to the author is forwarded but the publisher cannot, unless specifically instructed by the author, give out an address or phone number.

    Any Internet references contained in this work are current at publication time, but the publisher cannot guarantee that a specific location will continue to be maintained. Please refer to the publisher's website for links to authors' websites and other sources.

Llewellyn Publications
A Division of Llewellyn Worldwide, Ltd.
2143 Wooddale Drive, Dept. 0-7387-0762-7
Woodbury, MN 55125-2989, U.S.A.
www.llewellyn.com

Printed in the United States of America

Dedicated to the Love Goddess in all her forms,
but especially Aphrodite, Freya, and Oshun.
Thank you for all you have given me,
and may I never forget to be grateful.

This is also dedicated to her gifts to me,
Bella and Joshua,
the loves of my life.

CONTENTS

Introduction, ix

Introduction

"Aℓℓ acts of ℓove and pℓeasure are ɦer rituaℓs."

That single line from Starhawk's rendition of Doreen Valiente's version of Charles Leland's translation of *Aradia*, a book that Neopagans have claimed as a primary spiritual source, is quoted far and wide throughout the Pagan community as the guideline for sexual morality. The quote reflects the commitment to sexual honesty that has become a driving force in the greater Pagan culture. Although Paganism is made up of many smaller sects, all with differing ideals and theology, for the most part we as a demographic tend to be more sexually tolerant than other religions. It is for this reason that Paganism has, for example, a higher percentage of GLBT people than many other faiths. Similarly, it has begun to attract a higher percentage of polyamorous partners as well. We're one of the most tolerant religions around, and as such we get a lot of folks looking for a niche that won't reject them as "agents of the devil."

This has created a lot of curiosity and sometimes a good deal of suspicion in members of the Neopagan demographic who are traditionally monogamous. What is this polyamory thing about, they ask, and why is there an increasing amount of it happening in our community? Is it a good thing or a bad thing? Speculations abound; everyone who knows anyone who is polyamorous probably also knows someone who tried it and had it fail spectacularly. This is often used as an object lesson by those who disapprove of it. However, you can't properly criticize something that you know little or nothing about. This book was created to explain the nature of polyamory to the wondering onlookers.

It was also created to help polyamorous Pagans, or those who'd like to be polyamorous, discover what it means to be both poly and Pagan, and how one affects the other. Is there a way of being poly that is specific to Pagans? That was the question I asked when I started taking interviews for this book, and my answers were as varied—and as interesting—as the Pagan demographic itself.

What is polyamory? The word was coined in the 1990s by Morning Glory Zell (see appendix III with her original article, "A Bouquet of Lovers") as a way to describe nonmonogamous relationships that were based on honesty and affection rather than deception. The word means "many loves," but its exact parameters are not completely clearly defined, even by those who practice it. Some parts of its definition, however, are clearly and strongly held by everyone who engages in it. They are:

1. The practice of polyamory holds that it is not morally or ethically wrong to have sexual and/or romantic relationships with more than one consenting adult at a time and that one need not give up one partner in order to be intimate with another.

2. The practice of polyamory holds that it is morally and ethically wrong to deceive any partner about your activities with any other partner. Polyamory is not about deception; indeed, if there is a concept of "cheating" or "infidelity" in polyamory, it is usually lying or being deceptive about one's activities. Although some people may place limits on how much information they wish to have about their partners' sexual and/or romantic activities, the information must be available for the asking.

3. The practice of polyamory, like any other alternative sexual practice, must be engaged in only by people who have all given their informed consent. If someone did not consent to being polyamorous, the people involved need to work that out first.

4. The practice of polyamory generally holds that communication between all parties is a good thing and that the proper response to conflict is negotiation and compromise, not simply rage or abandonment.

5. The practice of polyamory, unlike that of simple nonmonogamy, holds that it is possible, and even desirable (depending on one's personal situation), to have not only more than one sexual relationship with someone, but more than one deeply loving and committed relationship. We hold also that loving one person does not necessarily "use up" all one's emotional depth and prevent them from loving another person equally deeply.

These are the basic tenets. This doesn't mean that there aren't arguments over these and other issues . . . there are, and we'll bravely tackle them all in the pages of this book. However, in general, the practice of polyamory sends a message of love and openness, not mere hedonism. "Most modern models of love function on a scarcity consciousness," says Brenna of Wisconsin, "just like most modern oppressive economic models function the same way. There's never enough love, so it must be hoarded and doled out only to one person at a time. Those of us who practice polyamory don't agree with this. We live our lives as if there was plenty of love to go around, and then some; a consciousness of abundance."

The Ravenhearts of California, the self-described "First Family of Polyamory," wrote vehemently to me about the joys of their lifestyle. "The freedom of having more than one devoted, bonded relationship is a joy that is almost impossible to describe to someone who has not experienced it. There is an inspiration to it, and amazing security. To us it is a human triumph of communication skills, moxie, romantic inspiration, and flexibility."

They also pointed out the similarity, as did many others, between the influx of GLBT people and poly people into the Pagan community. "We have long drawn an analogy between being polyamorous and being gay. Just as many people are naturally homosexual, so, we believe, are many people just naturally polyamorous. But in a culture in which being straight, or monamorous, is almost universally considered to be the only possible option (legally as well as culturally), people who don't fit that pattern must conduct their affairs in shameful secrecy. Thus, if one is going to act on those inclinations, 'cheating' is implicit. What we are trying to do is just what the gay community has been doing over the past few decades: that is, present the reality and validity of alternatives to what has been so long regarded as 'the norm.' And thus those who are truly poly in nature (just as those who are truly gay in nature) may understand themselves not as some kind of shameful sicko, but as merely another variation in the Goddess's delightful diversity of humanity. As in the fable of *The Ugly Duckling*, we just have to find the others who are like us."

Ruth in Massachusetts points out the fallacies in the idea that humans can only love one person: "When was I ever not poly? I loved my mother and my father as a child, loved my brother and sister as well! That set me off on a childhood and teenhood of not understanding why anyone should not love more than one person. By the time someone got around to explaining to me that I wasn't supposed to be involved with more than one person, well, I was already dealing with the idea that I wasn't supposed to be bisexual, and I ignored that too. Why should I listen to either? I mean, the same people who told me that I should 'play the field' and not 'tie myself down' to one person while dating in high school were now telling me that I could only marry one of these people? What!? Polyamory is like being a child and being able to love all four of your grandparents, or being a parent and being able to love all six of your kids. It's not a threat to monogamous people in any way, shape, or form. For me, polyamory isn't just about sex. It's more about washing the dishes, giving backrubs, and playing with the children and the kittens on the floor. Polyamory is about love, about inclusion, about building family, not tearing it down. Get it?"

Some people may have an idealistic, wistful version of polyamory in their heads, assuming that if one were a practicing polyamorist, finding people would be so much easier, because you wouldn't have to commit yourself to only one lover. Generally, the opposite seems to be true. "Nearly all monogamous people won't date you if you're polyamorous," was one comment. "Or if they do, they're doing it with their fingers crossed that you'll change for them, and when you don't, they dump you. It means that you can really only date other poly folks, and that significantly reduces your dating pool."

I asked everyone that I interviewed whether they felt that polyamory was simpler than monogamy. Most were firm about the fact that polyamory isn't easier at all, due to all the interpersonal issues that have to be worked out. Alex in Massachusetts agrees that "polyamory is a lot more difficult and complex than monogamy, but it can ultimately be so much more rewarding, and can become a tremendous source of security and support."

Others referred to polyamory as "grad school relationships" as opposed to "beginner relationships" and warned that it was best to work out major issues of insecurity and other serious emotional baggage with a single person before involving others in the mix. Jen from Boston says, "It is not an escape, a way to get out of the responsibilities that go along with monogamy. Yes, there are many benefits, but in many ways being polyamorous is harder than being monogamous. There are more people's wants, needs, assumptions, and emotional baggage to discuss, acknowledge, and deal with. It's my opinion that no one should attempt to be poly until they have demonstrated that they can first have a successful long-term relationship. Of course, I've broken that rule myself, but hey! I can still say it."

Some had leaped straight into polyamory in their teens, never even bothering with a monogamous relationship. "Sure, it sounds like a good idea to work out all that stuff before getting into multiple relationships," one such participant commented, "but I've always been incapable of being monogamous. Just trying to do it would create more problems for me—and the other person—than the safety of monogamy would solve. So I had to do it the hard way."

One of the things that you'll find in this book is a bank of rituals for polyamorous lovers to engage in together, as bonding activities or as practical rites of passage. You'll also find some spells—what's a Pagan book about any kind of love without a few love spells?—that are designed to be used in the case of emotional emergencies. All of them are, I believe, completely ethical when done as ordered. Most of them I've done myself. However, there are a few caveats to keep in mind when doing magic for any emotional purpose.

First, remember that you have a subconscious and that it may or may not want to be bound to whatever spell you're putting on yourself. If there is an unconscious (or semiconscious) part of yourself that doesn't want this spell, it will fight it. Its first battlefield will be the actual act of casting the spell. If you sit down to do one of these spells—especially the emotionally severe ones—and find your concentration wandering, or stray thoughts distracting you, or just a vague feeling of discomfort or dread, or any physical symptoms such as nausea, muscle cramps, headache, or strange twitching, stop. Go somewhere and meditate, and ask what part of yourself is resisting this, and why. The source of energy for doing magic comes out of your subconscious, and your subconscious is quite capable of sabotaging the casting itself, if there is serious internal dissent in your psyche.

This doesn't mean that there's no hope, only that you need to do some "know thyself" work before continuing. Take however long you need—hours, days, weeks—to work out what's going on in your own depths, and let that part of you speak through your mouth and air its grievances, if only when you're alone in your room. If you can negotiate with it, perhaps offering it something that it wants in exchange, great. If you can't, you're going to have to decide whether or not it's worth it to you to override it and just do the spell anyway. Sometimes hard things have to be done, and the more irrational, childlike, or beastlike parts of you protest because they can't understand the long view of things. In this case, you may just have to bite your tongue and do the work anyway, with the understanding that they will fight it, and that there's a chance they'll sabotage the working altogether. (If you're focused, though, you can force it through. Calling on patron deities to help is also useful; the word of a god/dess can override the stubbornest subconscious complaint, although that part of you may still be unhappy and act up in other ways.)

On the other hand, sometimes those irrational, childlike, or beast-like parts of you have a better handle on your emotional needs than your upper mind, and they are legitimately trying to tell you that you are about to walk blindly into something that will be psychologically damaging for you. This is especially true if you're the sort with a history of living in your head and not your guts, of going with your ideals instead of your feelings. It's hard to tell the difference. In these cases, a reading with a trusted diviner might be the best tactic.

These spells are here to help you, but they should only be used with care and forethought. Remember that binding yourself is just that: a bond, a chain, a weight, a restriction. Don't enter into it lightly. You might want to add a "term limit" to some of them, so that you have some hope of eventual escape if it turns out to be the wrong decision.

The quotes in this book were drawn from over a hundred questionnaires that were distributed over the Internet, at Pagan gatherings, at polyamorous support groups, at GLBT conferences, and at science fiction conventions. The multiple points of attack were meant to get a wide and varied cross section of this small, overlapping demographic. When you're dealing with a minority within a minority, it's difficult to get a whole lot of responses, and I considered myself lucky to have as many as I had. The folks in this book are real, impassioned, opinionated Pagans with a clear agenda: to make people understand that their lifestyle is a valid and functional alternative to ordinary monogamy.

I'm on that same wagon, and I admit it freely. Although I would never claim that polyamory is for everyone, or even for most people, I will not give credence to any claim that it is harmful or immoral in and of itself. It can be done wrong, of course, but then so can monogamy. The 50 percent divorce rate is proof of that. Although I do address the concerns of the anti-polyamory line, this book does not attempt to provide a "balanced" forum in which that attitude is given equal claim to correctness. (As one gay friend says about gay-bashing, "Screw the everyone's-point-of-view-is-right-in-some-way bull. Sometimes you're just plain wrong.") If you'd like to see such a book, write it yourself . . . if you can still convince yourself of it after reading this one cover to cover.

If you're reading this book because you're already polyamorous and Pagan, much of it may be old hat to you. Then again, it may not. One of the complaints that I got again and again was the lack of role models for polyfolk who are just starting out on their own. Although there are a few books on polyamory and how to do it, resources are still few and far between. The interest in the lifestyle is far outstripping the limited resources available and that includes people talking about how to do this in a practical way. Every time I've been to a polyamory workshop at a conference, convention, or gathering that was not in itself about polyamory, the room was completely full, sometimes even to the point of standing-room only, with people spilling out into the hallway. (These days, if I'm asked to be on a poly panel for such a convention, I make sure to let them know to put it in their largest possible room.) Everyone seems fascinated by it, including those who don't know anything and those who have fantasies of the perfect poly lifestyle.

So the moral of the story is: if you're openly polyamorous in the Pagan community, you're going to end up being a role model. People will be watching you. That doesn't mean that you cannot have troubles or break up. It does mean that it's in your best interest to speak honestly about what went wrong, and what you learned from it, and how you'll do things better next time. It also means that for those who are happily ensconced, you need to speak in practical terms about both the good stuff and the difficult parts and how you managed them.

If you're reading this book because you're interested in polyamory, this is a gift to you from those of us who are long-timers so that you may be prevented from making at least some of our mistakes. Nearly all of us have screwed up at least once, sometimes spectacularly. If our advice prevents even one massive, ugly breakup, we've done our job. Welcome to our tribe, and may you find joy in forming your own.

PART I

Air

The Ideal

The element of air is usually the first element that we call upon in Pagan ritual, because so many cultures mark the beginning of human life as the first breath of air into an infant's body. It is the element of mind, of ideas, of words and communication, and of stories. Relationships, too, go through the elemental round, and they start with air. Starhawk has characterized this early phase of a relationship as "the Telling of the Tales," where new partners reveal themselves through telling the stories of their lives, their interests, their worldviews, in order to compare and contrast and determine their compatibility.

In polyamory, the ideal often comes first, before the practice or the word. Perhaps someone hears about it and thinks, "Wow, that would certainly be more fun than how I'm doing it now!" They might also come to it on their own, imagining to themselves, "It would be great if I didn't have to be monogamous, but I don't want to cheat. How can I make this work, ethically? What would have to be going on in order to make it work?" By the time they stumble upon other poly people, they may already have their own system in place.

YuleCat in Massachusetts describes a fairly common process in coming to polyamory. "I was monogamous in my first serious relationship. I loved her, but I still felt the urge to see what else was out there, even though I was completely happy with her and our relationship. This led to me cheating on her a number of times. I lied about it, got away with it, and would have continued to get away with it in the future, but then I met a girl who actually mattered to me. We started forming an actual relationship while I was still involved with my previous girlfriend. It's easy to hide a one-night-stand, but not a second lover. I couldn't live with the guilt anymore, so I told her and, not surprisingly, it ended. Ironically, the other girl left me soon afterward. I guess that's karma for you. I spent the next six months sleeping around at Pagan gatherings, sowing my wild oats, and then one of my flings told me about polyamory . . . Initially, I saw this as a way to have a serious relationship and not get yelled at for having fun on the side as well, but over time the form and depth of our poly relationships became much more than that."

Most of the Pagans that I interviewed, however, came to polyamory by watching other people do it, often at a festival, convention, or other public Pagan event. Most of this group came to it through Pagan sources (although a few stumbled upon it at science fiction conventions) and thus absorbed it from a Pagan viewpoint, although what that meant to them was somewhat vague. Most of them also did their hunting for potential partners in a Pagan or semi-Pagan venue.

Some of the polyfolks that I interviewed were living with non-Pagan spouses and dealing with interfaith issues (which we'll deal with further in Part V). Others, like Ash in Massachusetts, vehemently prefer to restrict themselves to Pagans: "Someone once said that dating outside of your religion is like dating outside of your species. I tend to agree with them. I find that an underlying spiritual connection based on a mutual worldview is essential to my relationships." Judie in Wisconsin says, "Our poly family is made up entirely of goddess-worshipping women, and the spiritual component of our family is so important that I don't think we could welcome someone into our family if they didn't connect with that energy. I can't imagine I'd want someone who couldn't take part in our family rituals with a whole heart. It would leave them out of too many things that are bonding for us."

On the other hand, some cared more about their lovers' polyamorous status than their religion. Ruth in Massachusetts blithely recounts, "Some of my partners are or have been Pagan. Some were Jewish, some Christian, some laying claim to no faith. Two were Thelemites, two were LaVeyan-style Satanists, and there was one Buddhist in there, one Hindu, and one practitioner of Voudoun."

Issues of labeling often plague beginning polyfolks. Labels can be words of power in a very real magical sense; how we define our loved ones and their place in our lives is hard to sum up, and some-times it's hard to find the perfect one-word label that carries all the right connotations and none of the wrong ones. Some complain that every common label comes with some sort of unpleasant baggage. "Lover" sometimes feels too intimate for use among strangers. "Part-ner" can imply business as well as romantic partners and may have connotations of a live-in, shared-bank-account-and-mortgage kind of relationship. "Boyfriend" and "girlfriend" can have connotations of ephemerality, and if you have two partners who are equal in their status in your life, and one's labeled husband/wife and the other boyfriend/girlfriend, it's easy for others to assume that the marriage is the "real," lasting relationship and the other one's just a temporary fling. On the other hand, "boyfriend" and "girlfriend" do seem to be the labels of choice for secondary partners, not so much for the con-notation of ephemerality so much as the secondary priority of the relationship. If you are friendly with the families of poly lovers you aren't married to, or who aren't your primary partner, labels for them can be difficult as well. One woman refers to her boyfriend's family as her "out-laws," as opposed to her husband's "in-laws."

Some polyamorous people create their own labels and system, perhaps using personal symbolism or magical affinities. Moira Wolf in Arizona says, "I refer to Nite as my co-mate. We view ourselves as a 'pack' since we are all wolf spirits. Storm and I are the 'alpha pair'—we've been together the longest, we own a home, a business, and many investments. Nite is beta male, and he doesn't aspire to be alpha. He's just happy belonging."

One of the most common sets of polyamory terms is primary-secondary-tertiary, as in "This is Autumn, my primary partner, and this is Jean, my secondary." The titles are not assigned on the basis of how much you love someone or how worthy they are as a human; they're about which relationship takes priority. Often, the primary partners are legally married or at the very least their relationship has seniority. Sometimes they own a home together, or share a joint bank account, or are otherwise financially entangled. A few even label regular but entirely casual lovers as tertiaries.

Other polyfolks would rather not have a hierarchy among their lovers and abjure the primary/secondary system. Some use it guardedly; Ruth comments that "I hate the primary-secondary terms, but like many people who don't like it but have no other words, I sometimes use them." It has its positive sides and its pitfalls, which are discussed in the Saturn chapter on boundaries.

One interesting thing was the folks who don't limit their "poly families" only to people with whom they are having sex. Brenna in Wisconsin points out that "one of the great things about defining your family as poly is that you can more easily include loving friends. To me, polyamory means 'many loves' . . . and that's about people that I love, not just people that I'm currently screwing. My poly family includes my ex-lover with whom I am no longer sexual, but with whom I am still very close friends." Galadriel in Philadelphia writes of her "steadiest relationship, which is quite platonic. My best friend and I have a very intimate spiritual friendship but no sexual relationship, as he's a gay man and I'm predominantly interested in women. He understands me on a level no one else does, and I believe we have known each other in past lifetimes as well as this one. He's the closest in my life to what I'd call *Anam Cara*, unconditional love." Ruth in Massachusetts tells of "a girlfriend that I have been with on and off for seven years. I don't know if other people would count her because we haven't had any sex in years, but I count her and she counts me."

Others were less comfortable about the idea of seeing nonsexual relationships in the same category as lovers. "There's a new theoretical trend among some people, especially women, to lump anyone with whom they have some sexual tension into the pile labeled 'lovers,'" says Judie from Wisconsin, a lesbian in a polyfidelitous foursome. "These folks tend to say, '*Lover* isn't about sex, it's about who I love.' While that sounds romantic and all, I think it isn't healthy. It can make for some squishy boundaries that are easy to violate, and misunderstandings can crop up." Joshua in Massachusetts exclaims, "Ick! That's appalling. If I'm not physically intimate with someone, they are not my lover, and if they were to call me their lover just because they feel sexually attracted to me, or emotionally attached to me, I'd be terribly uncomfortable. It would feel like they were stalking me, pressuring me to make that relationship more than it is. It means that they would be defining what we were without my input and consent, and that's creepy."

Poly relationships can take many forms, and it's not uncommon to want to draw them out in a diagram. This is jokingly called "polygeometry" among polyfolk, and certain jargon labels have sprung up to express those alternative shapes. In the magical numerology of shapes, the dyad, or two points between a line, is the symbol of partnership, the heart of I-Thou. Certainly every polygeometry shape is made up of lines, just as every poly relationship is made up of a series of one-on-one partnerships, but what happens to the magical symbolism when you add more people?

The next step up from two is three, and the most common poly shapes have three points. Three is the number of magic, of Mercury, of the mind; it is both less stable than two—it's harder to change anything in a dyad, whereas a third party is always throwing the dyadic stasis off balance—and more stable, as it's the minimum number of points needed to make something stand firmly. This combination of stability and instability seems to be par for the course for the quicksilver, elusive number three . . . and for three-way relationships. They can be the extra leg that the couple needs to do more than they had ever dreamed, or they can be the catalyst that prods them into conflict . . . or both.

The most common configuration of polyamorous partners is a V, with one central person maintaining two sexual/romantic relationships with two people who are not sexually intimate with each other. The reason for its commonality seems to be that it's how people start taking baby steps into polyamory. Generally, one person decides that they'd like to try it, and their primary lover cautiously agrees, and they go out and find another lover . . . or they may have already fallen in love with someone and see polyamory as their only chance of having both partners at once. Because it's the most common "beginning" poly relationship, it's also the one with the most break-ups, usually either because the original partner underestimated how they would feel about seeing their partner with another lover, or because the person at the point of the V underestimated how difficult it would be to mediate between their two lovers.

It is a place of pressure, make no mistake. Being at the point of a V is the hardest role in polyamory, because it means that you have two people's full-time attention and needs focused on you. It means that you may be expected to mediate between them, and perhaps less focus is placed on their ability to communicate, because of course you're there, and you've learned to speak both their languages, and since they're both there for you, why should they bother to have much of a relationship with each other? How healthy this is will vary depending on many factors: how much time is spent with each of them, whether there is a clear primary and secondary, whether you move in the same social circles, whether you live far apart or near each other or even all together. If one partner is your full-time live-in primary and the other is an occasional lover that you see once in a while in a different state, then the need for the two of them to communicate regularly on their own or have a strong independent relationship may not be relevant. On the other hand, if you are all trying to live together, and/or if you are juggling two primary partners, their ability to communicate other than through you may be crucial to keeping things clear and aboveboard.

I think of a V relationship as a glyph of a human being raising their arms to the sky. Each outstretched hand holds the life of one lover, one person who is special to them. When you stand like that, with your arms toward the sky, the point that is central to your two arms is your heart, and this too is symbolic. If you are the focal point of a V relationship, your heart is what is binding them together. If lightning strikes one or both of your hands, it will run through your heart. Similarly, any conflict between your lovers will rip through your heart, and this is the price that you will pay for being the center point.

One hand may be held closer to your heart and one perhaps further away. However, when you experience pain in one of your hands, the first thing that you do is to bring that hand, instinctively, close to your heart chakra. This works for lovers as well; when one of them is hurting, your instinct is to gather them into yourself. To keep both lovers in balance with each other is a continual, conscious dance in which you must think three times before doing any action: once for yourself and once for each lover.

Sometimes a V can evolve into a triangle, where all three members are intimately involved with each other to some extent, or a couple can deliberately look for someone who will be lovers with both of them. This can be even trickier than when one person seeks a compatible partner, especially if they're attracted to different people. If the other partner gets a second partner, the V can become a W or a square if they both get involved. Care must be taken with a square, however, that it not pull away into two dyads. Squares, being ruled by the number four, the sign of stability, can be stronger than triangles if the relationships are all good. Having a four-person relationship means that processing isn't as likely to be perceived as two people "ganging up" on one other hapless soul, and if three are ganging up on one, they may be more likely to believe them through sheer numbers.

Another configuration is the "line marriage." Although it can vary somewhat from its classical definition, the "traditional" line marriage consists of a committed chain of individuals, each with one to two relationships linking them together. (Bob is with Celia, who is also with Joe, who is also with Pixie, who is also with Brian, who is also with Jeannine, etc.) In some cases—for example, where a group line marriage has a family purpose, such as maintaining a piece of land or an organization—there may often be significant age differences between partners, bringing "new blood" into the group or having younger members take care of older members as they age. A line marriage also implies a high level of commitment; similar configurations that are more casual are usually just referred to as "chains." Some are not so clear and linear; the Ravenhearts of California describe their line marriage as "each person is linked into the group by one or more intimate relationships, but not necessarily with everyone else. Visualize a molecular diagram!"

No matter what the geometric configuration, each separate relationship within the system needs to be taken into account and nourished separately. A Pagan triad in Massachusetts explains: "We definitely have four relationships in one. There's Wintersong and Fireheart; there's Wintersong and Summerwind; there's Fireheart and Summerwind; and our whole relationship, which is considered to be the dominant force. We all took the same last name—Tashlin—and we refer to that fourth relationship as Tashlin, as in 'Tashlin wants . . .' or 'Tashlin does . . .'"

Meeting polyamorous lovers is much easier said than done. As we've already pointed out, becoming poly limits rather than expands your dating pool, so one has to look a lot further to find someone with compatible values. Some Pagans look online, on poly email lists or websites; some check out ads in poly magazines, but the majority seem to go to Pagan gatherings, cruise various interesting people, and weed out the monogamous ones. Others look in polyamorous support and dating groups, which tend to be centered in urban areas. A word of warning, however; some of these groups encourage dating, and others (like Family Tree in the Boston area) are strictly support and discussion groups who stress that they are not a venue for cruising. If your first priority is finding partners, make sure that you find out the nature of any given group and don't violate their etiquette.

"Bring Me Polyamorous Love" Spell

What would a Pagan book on love be without a love spell? Here's one just for us, to ask the Divine Bureau of Human Resources—otherwise known as the love deities—to give us the kind of love we're looking for.

Start with a large pillar candle of the proper color. If you're looking for passionate, highly sexual love, use red. If it's for a long-term romantic relationship, use pink. If your prime need is for someone who will live with you in your home as part of a family and possibly bear and/or raise children with you, use green for earthy bonds and growth. (Of course, if there's another color that has special meaning for you and that seems particularly right, go with your own intuition.) In some candle stores you may find really big candles with multiple wicks; these are especially appropriate for this spell.

If you can, put together a mix of essential oils that are related to love, such as rose, violet, apple blossom, etc. (If you really want the definitive guide to love oils, check out the book *Handfasting and Wedding Rituals: Inviting Hera's Blessing* [Llewellyn, 2003], which has more information on that sort of thing than you'll ever need.) Each person involved in the spell should get oil on their fingers. If there are more than one of you, start by anointing each other and affirming your love and/or friendship, depending on the various bonds in the circle of people. Then each person anoints the candle, saying, "I come to the flame of love with an open heart."

Each person involved in the spell should have acquired one or more lengths of colored thread, at least a yard long and preferably more. The colors of each one should represent a trait that they want in the new lover—for instance, blue for intelligence, orange for humor, brown for the ability to actually hold a real job, red for a high sex drive (or pale pink for a low one), and so forth. There's no real rule on what colors represent what traits; this is an intensely personal spell and an intensely personal request, and the best color associations will be intuitive and personal rather than traditional. Your own psyche has to be all right with this.

If there is more than one person involved and the new lover will hopefully be involved with some or all of them, it's especially good karmic points to ask for traits that will aid them in being a good lover for your other lover(s), such as, "This bright purple thread represents that hope that this new person will share some of Stone's hobbies, especially the ones I'm not interested in," or "This pale green thread represents the compassion and understanding that I want this new lover to have for Chris's disability," or "This silver thread symbolizes Shawna's silver hairs and my hope that our new lover will find her beautiful in spite of any age gap."

Each person ties one end of their thread around the very bottom of the pillar candle. (Although you can have as many threads as you want, it's good not to fill up more than the bottom third of the candle, because you will be burning it down.) The other end of each thread gets loosely tied around the left wrist of the person who brought it, in a big enough loop that they can easily slip their hand out. The querent(s) stand around the candle, tied to it by the threads, and one person lights the candle, saying, "We are blessed with the presence of the flame of love." Each person then recites the following prayer, either one after the other or as a call-and-response with one person reading it off and the others reciting it back.

Lady of Love who dances in our hearts,

We call you to this place

In the heart of this dancing flame.

Love flows in this circle in abundance,

Enough and more for many lovers,

And we wish to share it still further.

You who are the magnetism of the universe,

Draw the right lover to these open arms,

And help us to trust in your decision.

You who are the spark of passion,

Let this yearning be a siren call

Heard only by the right ears.

Let it be a song in their blood,

A voice in the wind,

That brings them to the light of this circle

And into the love of a family.

We swear that here in this place,

Their unique soul will be appreciated

And the song of their heart desperately needed

To match, and to complement,

The songs that are sung here tonight.

Everyone takes the threads off of their wrists and wraps the remaining lengths around the candle. It should be allowed to burn down to the point where the threads begin. If this takes several days, it is acceptable to carefully put it out and relight it again the next morning. Once the candle is burned to that point, it should be carefully wrapped in cloth and put somewhere safe where it will not be lost. During the period that it is burning, if possible, the spellcasters should play music (by themselves if they're musicians, otherwise break out the tapes and the CDs and the stereo or boom box) and sing along to it. The songs chosen should be everyone's favorite love songs; ransack your collection for the ones that move you the most. Sing along with them, dance to them, and generally have a love-song festival for the next hour or so. This is your offering to the Love Goddess, so do it up.

If she's happy with your offering, she'll send someone over. However, it may take a long time—days, weeks, perhaps even months or a year or two, especially if you've made a lot of very specific requests. That doesn't mean that it's bad to be picky, only that it takes somewhat longer for Divine HR to process the request properly. However, we've seen some truly amazing partnerships happen with the direct help of the Love Goddess. Just make sure when they show up in your life that you are paying enough attention to recognize them and to sign for the package.

Mercury

Communication, Communication, Communication!

A strologically, Mercury is the planet of words and motion. Mercury talks, writes, orates, reads, researches, thinks, and runs around very fast. Mercury's primary job is to communicate thoughts and ideas as quickly and as precisely as possible.

In polyamory, good communication is more than just a nice idea, it's as necessary as food and breathing. Without it, the whole thing falls apart. The problem is that most people aren't taught good communication skills, especially when it comes to talking about tricky emotional subjects. There's a cultural myth that lovers are just supposed to know each other's thoughts, to sense what's wrong, and to automatically figure out the right thing to do about it. This was summed up once by a "Cathy" cartoon I saw. The main character is complaining to her best friend about her boyfriend: he doesn't have enough of this quality or that quality; she'd rather he was like this or like that; she wants someone who does this or that. After each complaint, her friend asks if she's said anything to him about his behavior, and she admits that she hasn't. At the end of the litany of complaints, her friend asks in exasperation how she expects him to change if she won't tell him what she wants. Her answer: "I want him to be a better guesser."

To make matters more difficult, some people are raised to stand up for what they want and get in people's faces about it, while others are discouraged from asking for anything and are taught that they should be quiet and be grateful for whatever they get. The former type tend to override the latter type without even noticing, and the latter type tend not to point it out until they've been seething with resentment a good long time. This sort of thing, perhaps coupled with the occasional "I'm fine," followed by a heavy sigh, can be the staple interaction of the average two-person relationship. Just watch any sitcom and count up the number of times where dishonesty or lack of communication between characters is not only central to the plot, but seems to be an accepted model of relationships: "This is just the way that marriages are. People are just like this with each other, and all we can do is to laugh about it so that we don't cry."

First of all, I don't believe that relationships have to be that way. I believe that they often end up that way due in part to lack of good relationship skills and in part to personal neuroses that get in the way of intimacy. There is, however, the problem that a dyad is a static situation. Two people have the ability to assiduously ignore the reality of a situation, and refuse to properly communicate, for an appallingly long time . . . possibly until one of them gets old and dies. When you add something to that dyad, it is no longer stable. (That's why having children can be like plastic explosives to a shaky relationship; it adds a third—or fourth, or fifth—party to the mix.) It's why we like dyads and why we tend to "revert" to them under stress, such as the middle of a fight. ("Well, Jenny's on my side, at least!") They are the most stable form of relationship and also the most prone to stagnation, rigidity, and self-delusion.

When adding another adult lover, you run the risk that they will see something about your current relationship that you can't see because your objectivity is lacking in this area. A good new lover will try to offer this information in as helpful a way as possible, taking care not to indulge any wishes that this might cause a breakup. (Actually, if you're the new lover and you're starting to wish for your new partner to break up with their spouse, you might want to be rethinking the whole relationship. Being a homewrecker is no fun, and if they're having serious marital problems, you don't want to be in the middle of that. Take a vacation while they work out their issues.) When done properly, being polyamorous can help give perspective on all your relationships. For example, if you don't really believe it when your spouse complains about a particular fault, sometimes hearing it from a new partner who has a different perspective can help you to understand your spouse's complaint.

Threes and fours and fives are less stable than dyads, because they contain more variables and there's a wider range of unexpected things that could knock over a stagnant stasis. Sometimes people even seem to seek out new relationships in a sort of unconscious need to upset their own applecarts, to break down the rigid walls that have grown up between themselves and their spouse/lover(s), which somehow they can't manage to do on their own. Regardless of whether this kind of blind stumbling is wise, they have one thing right: the more people you add to the dynamic, the shorter the time period that denial will be tolerated and communication blocked off.

As Pagans, we have (or we ought to have) a commitment to introspection and self-knowledge, to digging out the dark places in our psyches. The problem is that sometimes we can't see into those places very well on our own, or we have built-up defenses that keep us "safe" from ourselves. Emotional processing isn't fun for most people, but it's not only vitally important if you want any kind of a poly relationship to survive, it's good for you. Alex in Massachusetts points out that becoming skilled in polyamory can be a good way to increase one's people skills and is useful in creating group coherence. "Besides the intimate bonds that it creates between lovers, it also develops a great deal of experience in developing intimacy with others. Another benefit with polyamory is that you quickly become an expert in conflict resolution." (In the resources section, appendix IV, you'll find books on communicating that various polyfolk have found useful.)

One poly Pagan listed the biggest communication problems she'd run into on her fingers. "First: just not talking. Thinking that things will resolve themselves on their own. (But Bullwinkle, that trick never works!) Second: sandbagging. Stuffing your feelings down and saying, 'Oh, yeah, everything's fine,' when it isn't. Maybe you're embarrassed because you have feelings you can't control; maybe you're afraid that you're going to rain on everyone's parade. Do it anyway. If they really love you, they'll listen. Third: lying. 'Nuff said. Fourth (and this is a tough one): lying to yourself."

Some poly groups have elaborate and specific guidelines for communication, especially ones where there are four or more participants who all live together in one house. "We get together once a week for family meetings," says Judie from Wisconsin, who lives with three lovers in a polyfidelitous lesbian foursome. "Every other week, the issue is practical household things—whose turn it is to pay the electric bill, who forgot to change the cat box, and so forth. Because we're also a self-contained coven and worship group, we also discuss issues of upcoming ritual at that time—last night we discussed our household Samhain ritual and how we wanted to go about it and how we could schedule it so as not to conflict with the local public circle. And every meeting between these household meetings is strictly about emotional processing. We've found that you need to leave the entire evening for these meetings, because they always take a lot longer than you expect. Don't start too late, or you'll be up till the wee hours and some people will be nodding off while others will be saying stupid things that they'll regret. Oh, and have food and drink to ground people while they're discussing heavy stuff, and 'fiddly' toys to twiddle or soft things to hug while they're saying hard things."

Some poly groups use roundtables, or talking sticks, or other structured ways to communicate during meetings. Some even report doing most of their arguments over email. The drawbacks were "that you couldn't see the expressions of everyone else, and you might miss subtleties, but by this time we know each other well enough that we can see the person in our minds saying the words on the screen. And it's outweighed by the usefulness of having every-thing down in writing, where no one can say that they didn't say this or that. Since none of us live together, and all three of us work jobs where we're on computers for most of the day, it's easier to work things out this way than to waste the precious face-time that we get with each other. We might as well be arguing via email in little cubi-cles while things download."

Rachel, Gio, and JT in Florida all use standard formal debate prac-tices when arguing. "We were all on debate teams in our various high schools," says Rachel, "and we love a good argument. Our shared love of formal debate helps us to feel like a team, even when we're battling it out. Sometimes that method doesn't work, like when the topic is so emotional that people are breaking down and crying, and then we have to just stop and hold each other, and talk quietly."

Other polyfolk don't bother with strict processing guidelines. PolyPagan of the Waterkin (his preferred name for this book) from New Zealand reports that "openness and honesty are our key essen-tial principles and guideposts. Nothing extreme, nothing radical; just plain open and honest as best we can, and apologizing when we slip up. Our communication evolves organically, like good cheese."

Oberon Zell-Ravenheart of California says, "How do the Raven-hearts deal with problems? By sitting down and talking them through (several members of the family are highly trained and skilled media-tors); by regular family meetings and planning/scheduling sessions; and by intense late-night conversations in bed or hot tub. If we can't handle a problem within our own family, we don't hesitate to call in outside mediators, or even, if we feel they can be helpful, see sympa-thetic professional therapists or marriage counselors."

Finding such sympathetic professionals to help you with your poly relationship is more difficult than just calling up a counselor out of the Yellow Pages, however. One psychiatrist that I spoke to compared the situation to that of gay people thirty years ago: "Two men would come in saying, 'We need to work on our relationship,' and the therapist would say, 'You're both sick, you shouldn't even be having this relationship, go out and get wives.' Which isn't helpful for anyone, but the psychiatric community didn't understand what healthy gay relationships looked like. Things changed when serious studies were done comparing queer people in long-term relationships with straight people who'd been together for the same period of time, and found that the queers weren't any mentally unhealthier than the heterosexuals. If any sexual subculture wants to convince the greater psychiatric community that they're just as healthy as anyone else, they'll have to do the same thing—rigorous studies by a reputable researcher. That's what convinces counselors that this lifestyle is worth learning more about, so that you can more adequately counsel them."

One possible option is to check out Kink Aware Professionals (KAP), found online at http://www.bannon.com/kap/. These folks specialize in finding people who are willing to work with folks of many different sexual minorities and alternative lifestyles. One of the positive things about KAP is that they list medical doctors as well; it's good to have doctors who are sympathetic to the fact that you have more than one spouse who wants visiting privileges. Another option is to check out the lists of poly-friendly professionals on the Loving More site (http://www.lovemore.com).

Being Pagan adds another layer of difficulty to the problem, especially if one follows some of the more esoteric Pagan traditions. Coming in with multiple spouses and a strange religion can trigger the word "cult" in the mind of some human services workers, especially those that have been overexposed to lurid tales of Satanic abuse. (More on this in the Moon chapter.) Convincing them that you're just ordinary people may be difficult. Frankly, if they seem nervous, edgy, or negative about your self-description, I'd go somewhere else. You don't need to be reeducating someone who is already biased against you while you're dealing with painful emotional issues of your own.

Not all Pagan clergy or Pagan therapists are able to deal with polyamory, either. One Pagan therapist that I know openly admits that she will not counsel polyamorous people because of her own irrational biases; she was dumped by a spouse who decided that he could no longer be monogamous, and she feels that her bitterness on the subject would interfere with her ability to adequately serve her clientele. Although I was saddened by her statement, I also felt that it was honest and useful—if you can't serve a particular client for whatever reason, it's best to be straight up about it before they waste their time and money. One could wish that all other helping professionals would be so quick to admit their biases.

Some Pagan poly families have had luck looking for other polyfolk in the Pagan community who are skilled in mediation rather than outright counseling. If your problems are communication-oriented rather than deeply emotional, mediation is a good option. A well-trained mediator will come to any situation as neutral and objective as they can possibly be, and most trained mediators have learned to deal with more than two people at a time. If there's an issue with the perceived biases of the mediator, it's possible to have two mediators present who are willing to work together. A good mediation session can give you a facilitation template for doing it by yourselves in the future.

The most important point for any kind of communication is to go into it with the attitude that things can be changed for the better and that you and the other people are all on the same side, working together to make those changes, or should be. Don't let the first blast of hostility or pain make you snap instantly into an adversarial position. Keep your own head centered on the team ideal. Keep saying, "What can we do to make sure that all our needs are met to at least some extent?" If you've already said it aloud too many times, say it to yourself, over and over.

Although hiding from issues is always the wrong way to go about things, sometimes being apart from the problem—and from each other—for a few hours or days or weeks can breathe new perspective into it, as well as giving everyone space to develop enthusiasm for more processing. Sometimes the horse is just dead, and beating it isn't as useful as giving it time to come to life again and get back into harness. Knowing when it's time for everyone to take a break from deep processing, and when it's just a request to flee, takes practice to figure out, though. This is especially difficult when people have different tolerances for processing or different levels of skill at communicating. Don't use your ability to process things as a weapon to beat someone with, showing them how bad they are at it. If they're feeling like that, you're not doing a good job anyway. The best communicators can help poor communicators develop better talking skills in the middle of the argument, aiding them in being articulate rather than just running over them with their own flash and polish.

Good communication takes practice and skill, but once you've mastered it, you can bring it to the table as a bonus for all your future relationships. It's worth it.

Communication Ritual to Open Polyamorous Family Meetings

The following ritual and invocation is used to create sacred space before a polyamory processing session. Ideally, it ought to help foster the creation of space where everyone feels heard and acknowledged, and where people think clearly about what they want to say before they say it, and where everyone is as honest and open as they can be.

Because the invocation calls on the powers of air, the ritual needs to start—before any unnecessary word is spoken—with a group breathing exercise. Everyone should sit comfortably, at whatever distance to each other they prefer, ideally facing each other in some sort of circle, oval, or general squiggle. Breathe in through the nose and out through the mouth, slowly and deeply. Sync your breathing together as a group, until you have all been breathing in unison for at least five minutes. If someone begins to cough or hyperventilate or otherwise get out of step, don't call it a failure and quit. Start again, letting them get what recovery time they need to jump back in. If you can't even supportively cooperate in breathing together, you have little hope of making a polyamorous discussion work.

At the end of this group breathing, you can go straight into the invocation or, if the family is inclined, you can add a musical note to your breath and all sing it in unison or harmony. Then the invocation is spoken, piece by piece. You can dole out the parts beforehand to those who have favorite verses, or just go around in a circle, or one person can read the whole thing. This is sometimes necessary with shy folks, but it works much better at creating space if it is shared. There's something about actually hearing your voice saying the words that drives home a commitment to fairness and honesty in the procedure.

COMMUNICATION INVOCATION

The center space is laid with a fan, a knife, and a talking stick. First, all share in a breathing exercise together. Then the first individual speaks:

> *Hail, powers of air!*
> *You are the breath in our bodies,*
> *The same breath shared by each of us,*
> *Without which there can be no life.*

We come before you strong in our knowledge

That we are on the same side together,

That we are bound by love and are not enemies,

That the happiness of one is key to the happiness of all.

Breathe in and know that this is true.

Hear us, powers of air!

The second speaker takes up the fan and gently fans the next person in the circle. The second person takes the fan and fans the next individual, and so it is passed until everyone has received the gift of wind. While this is going on, the second speaker says:

Hail, powers of air!

You are the wind of change

That blows through our minds.

We come before you open to changing

If that is what is necessary

To keep a balance strong between us.

We will not fear change,

Even when it is less than comfortable,

For you are the power of the rising sun,

The glory of dawn,

And all new beginnings.

Hear us, powers of air!

The third speaker takes up the knife between their two hands and presses it reverently to their third eye, and then passes it on. Each in turn repeats the gesture, while the third speaker says:

Hail, powers of air!

You are the knife's edge,

Separating one thing from another,

Untangling the threads of our knotted feelings.

We come before you ready to feel your edge,

Even when it cuts deep,

For the sharp glance of another may see

What we have hidden from ourselves.

And yet we promise not to abuse that edge,

Nor to slash carelessly at each others' souls,

So that every cut made is the surgeon's scalpel,

Taken into the service of healing

Rather than destruction.

Hear us, powers of air!

The fourth speaker picks up the talking stick and says:

Hail, powers of air!

You are the power of words,

The song of meaning,

The stream of communication,

The many stories of language.

We swear to try our best

To learn each others' language,

That understanding may always flow between us.

Gift us with the knowledge of the perfect word,

The perfect phrase, the right thing

That will resolve each argument

And yet not stifle the flow of feeling

From whence it sprang.

Hear us, powers of air!

The fourth speaker then says:

> *I come to this circle speaking only truth,*
>
> *Holding forth only hope,*
>
> *Seeing only friends,*
>
> *And giving each their say.*

Each person, as they take the talking stick for the first time, should repeat this short verse. The discussion can now commence in whatever order the polyamorous family prefers.

PART II

Fire

The Passion

The element of fire is the spark of energy within us. It can ignite into sexual passion, or burning need, or righteous anger, or destructive rage, or the will to burn through all obstacles. It is the second stage of relationships, after the stage of air where we tell our stories and dream our airy dreams. In the fire stage, our love flares high, and we fight over power. The majority of new relationships break up in this stage, as people discover through struggle that they are unsuitable for each other. In polyamory, struggle is an accepted part of the deal, or it should be. Just as passion will flare, so will tempers. The difference is that one can choose where to put that struggle: do we focus it on our partners or on our obstacles as a team? Dousing the fire of a relationship will cause it to fizzle out. It's better to find a useful place to aim that fire.

One thing that people can fall in love with is the ideal of polyamory itself. For many of the participants that I interviewed, even if their first poly experiment didn't work, they felt so strongly about their new lifestyle that they simply got up and tried again. "Having tasted what it's like to live in this poly family," says Judie of Wisconsin, "I could never be monogamous again, except by default, and then I'd be unhappy. Even if all my lovers broke up with me tomorrow, I wouldn't give up on this lifestyle. It satisfies something deep inside me. My passion is bigger than any one person can hold. So I'm a polyamorous activist; I fight for our right to be what we are. In the lesbian community where I mostly hang out, this isn't easy; women are socialized to think that monogamy is romantic, which I think is a holdover from breeding and being dependent on a man. So when I'm irrationally angry at my lovers, I turn that anger against the pressures of society that refuse to accept us."

For some, falling in love with the ideal of polyamory is hanging their hopes on a fragile, unrealistic bubble that is quickly shattered. For others, it's a commitment to an ideal, and it helps them keep going in the face of emotional struggle. Passion can be channeled many different directions, in the same way that one forces electricity through shielded wires in order to make it useful. To place your passion in the service of making your relationships work is to acknowledge the value not only of your lovers, but of your belief that this lifestyle is just as workable—and as sacred—as any traditional monogamous relationship.

So what sustains passion in polyamorous relationships? I asked many polyamorous folks their thoughts on the best and the worst things about polyamory, and mostly I got the same few answers, such as:

"In our opinion, the best thing about being poly is knowing that there are two people in the world who love you for yourself above all else. Splitting up chores ain't bad either."

"More interpersonal opportunities to have fun with people you like, and little time for boredom! Being able to build loving relationships with more than one person, and have it given back to you."

"We're always in 'date mode.' Since we're seeing other people, we tend to maintain the dating mindset, which means that we don't get bored with each other and lose our spark."

"I admit it—at first I was in it for sex with multiple partners without getting in trouble for it like I did when I was cheating. But the appeal of that wore off for me, especially when I started forming meaningful bonds with my partners. One fulfills parts of my life that the others don't, and can't, because they're different people. And I find that new lovers fulfill areas that I never realized I wanted. These days, I'm not so much in it for the sex—although I'll be the first to say that it's great with all of them—but for the relationships."

One of the most-quoted reasons was the idea that you can't get everything you need from only one lover, because they're human beings and, by definition, limited. "There's this myth that we're all taught that you'll find the One Perfect Lover who can fulfill you in every way, but it's just a myth," storms Brenna from Wisconsin. "Even if you have a wonderful lover, there will be holes where the two of you have incompatible needs. Instead of berating them for not being something they're not, it's better to appreciate what they can give you, and go get the other needs filled elsewhere."

Moira Wolf in Arizona concurs: "My relationships are complex. Storm and I are friends, first and foremost; we are legally married and co-owners of a business. But while we are lovers, he's not the toucher-feeler that I am; never has been. He tried for years to be what I needed, but it just wasn't him. We are mates, we are partners, but we are not passionate lovers. He is not very physically driven; he has very little sex drive. I'm the wild one, with a high libido. Nite fits that side of me much better; we're very touchy and snuggly . . . So I have the best of both worlds. I have strength and dependability in Storm, and passion and softness in Nite. I don't have to depend on Nite and his business sense (he has none!), and I don't have to go to Storm for my touch-fix for the day (he doesn't like spending hours doing nothing but snuggling)."

The Ravenhearts of California agree: "It's a great freedom to know that if one intimate is not available or able to meet our needs, someone else is. Conversely, we are aware that someone else can meet our lover's needs if we are unable or unwilling. Theoretically, many needs can be met by people we don't have sex with, but in fact the erotic bonding gives us deeper access to the nourishment another human being can provide."

Galadriel in Philadelphia says, "The best thing about polyamory is not having to place a limit on how many relationships I can have (except via time restraints). It means that I don't have to say, 'You can only be my friend and nothing more,' or even 'You can only be my fuckbuddy and nothing more.' It allows my relationships to develop to their fullest potential over time in whatever way they end up developing. Plus it's amazing how much love you can share with more than one person if you are free to do so."

When it came to the worst things about polyamory, there were very few categories of response, but the same problems kept cropping up again and again. I've chosen to call these the Demons of Polyamory. They are divided into two categories, the Greater Demons and the Lesser Demons, depending on how personalized their venue is. The Lesser Demons require more internal work on the self, while the Greater Demons work most of their wiles in the other world. Banishing them is a difficult thing, but I have given instructions on how to start. None of the directions for banishing is likely to work immediately; they will take a great deal of work—especially for some of the Greater Demons, which may take a lifetime of work to exorcise. Still, it's worth doing. Here, then, is the *Demonologia Polyamoria!* Welcome, and brace yourself.

(Disclaimer, disclaimer! My secondary lover points out that some people reading this may think that I'm actually talking about real demons and real demonology. I'm not. This is all tongue in cheek, all right? The spells, however, are quite real and will work just fine. Got it? Are you with me? Then let's proceed.)

Demonologia Polyamoria

THE GREATER DEMONS

I. The Pariah Factor

The single biggest problem for respondents seemed to be the pain of lack of social acceptance. A Massachusetts triad admits that "the worst thing has been dealing with our families and the general world about our relationship. Obviously, ours is not an overly accepted way of life, which makes it necessary to hide it from many people, which at this stage in our lives is difficult."

Sometimes the level of "outness" depends on the conservative nature of the local community. Moira Wolf says that "within the Pagan community, I am openly poly. In my mundane business, I'm not . . . To everyone other than Pagans, Nite is 'a friend.' Which hurts; he's so important to me. I *hate* lying about our relationship; it cheapens and degrades it in my eyes, but I can't be open. Hell, this town tried to run me out of the local street fair for Tarot reading."

Galadriel in Philadelphia has similar complaints. "The worst thing about polyamory is that society doesn't understand it or accept it. I am open and uncloseted about my political beliefs, spiritual beliefs, and sexual preference, but I'm not completely out about poly because most people wouldn't understand that I'm not an adulterer even though my boyfriend is married. I suppose if I was dating other singles this would be easier to understand—a twenty-something female dating around and playing the field—but dating a married man, well, most people would not be thrilled with that concept, even if open marriage was not foreign to them."

This demon whispers things like, "What are you doing? You can't tell your parents about this lifestyle, or your grandparents, or your friends. You'll be disowned. If people in your neighborhood find out, you'll be ostracized. Their kids won't be allowed to play with your kids. You'll never be able to legally marry your other lovers. Everyone will think that you're an adulterer and a terrible person. They'll never believe that your partner is fine with it; they'll just think that you're pressuring them into it. Do you really want to get into a situation where you'll have to keep your love life closeted?"

To Exorcise the Pariah Factor Demon: This is the greatest and most powerful demon of all, and its exorcism will take the combined efforts of every polyamorous person on the planet. It isn't an easy task, either. You'll have to come out of your closet and be counted; talk about polyamory to anyone who asks you; form educational groups and lobby for your rights; and in general do all the things that other sexual minorities are already doing. If you're at a loss as to where to start, contact those other sexual minority groups and ask for advice. (See the resources appendix in the back of this book.) This demon will not be banished without all our efforts.

II: The Time-Cruncher

The second most frequent complaint was about the lack of time. Alex in Massachusetts admits that "scheduling is a problem. Being polyamorous is very time-consuming." YuleCat complains about the issue of "time management. With both of us working full-time jobs to survive, we see little of each other as it is. We literally have to book one night each week specifically for each other to the exclusion of all else, because if we don't, we won't see each other at all. My secondary lives over an hour away, which makes evening visits after work difficult. My new lover is more than two hours away and does not have a car, making it impossible for me to see her except on weekends. So far I seem to have balanced everyone pretty well, but there's always the possibility that someone may feel left out in favor of someone else, which is something I really don't want to do."

The time-cruncher demon likes to play on your guilt. "You aren't spending enough time with any of your lovers. They're all going to start complaining about how you don't love them enough to give them enough attention. How can you possibly hold down this lifestyle and still have a life? Better to give up now before it all comes crashing down."

To Exorcise the Time-Cruncher Demon: Get more organized. Buy calendars and datebooks and use them. Let go of the idea that "it isn't romantic unless it's spontaneous," or at least block large amounts of time specifically for spontaneity. Make sure that you're actually spending quality time with people, doing something that you both like. On the other hand, I've had a good time just going to the grocery store with a lover, so try incorporating them into ordinary activities, if that's their thing, and they won't be bored and insulted. Remember that polyamory is a costly lifestyle—not in money, but in time. Don't take on more than you can handle, or you'll find yourself deep in romantic debt with your relationships, declaring bankruptcy. Be realistic about what your life can currently handle. And while you're at it, get a good long-distance phone program, especially if you have lovers living outside your local calling area.

III. What's All This Processing Nonsense?

Other complaints were about the constant level of processing needed to keep poly relationships healthy. Ash in Massachusetts groans about "having to deal with more than one person on the icky personal things that you wouldn't talk about with non-lovers. But those things also mean that they trust and love you enough to share that part of themselves with you, and that's very empowering."

The Ravenhearts of California offer their insights on coping with the stresses of polyamory. "Our problems basically revolve around overstimulation and cascading episodes of stress. Sometimes it might be a flu or cold bug; sometimes an overdose of emotional intensity; sometimes one person has a crisis and in the middle of it another one has a crisis. What do you do then? The good news is that you have more resources to deal with these situations, and if you need a break or even a change in lifestyle, the system is flexible enough to bend quite a bit without breaking. We don't have to break up with someone in order to change our relationship; we can stay in the intimate connection and change its form. So polyamory can be very evolutionary in that way."

Of course, some people had a lot of experience with poly relationships that had gone awry, and they spoke about how bad things could get emotionally when people weren't as honest and straight-forward as they'd promised. Ruth in Massachusetts mourned: "The worst thing has been the petty backstabbing, and the pain when two gang up on one. I remember when I was a child, two kids playing went well, four kids or more playing went well, but three was always a danger because two would almost always gang up on one. That's why I don't like threesomes, and I prefer to live with a larger poly family."

This particular demon especially loves to plague people who aren't well-trained in expressing their feelings or who are uncomfortable with feelings in general. It whispers, "Do you really want to talk about all that embarrassing stuff with all those people? All your dark secrets will come out and they'll laugh or be disgusted, and they won't want you for a lover anymore. Or, even worse, they'll tell you that you have to change. This is public humiliation. It's not worth it. Just keep quiet and nod and smile, and they'll go on about their own feelings and not notice that you're not talking. And with luck, you can excuse yourself before nine when your favorite TV show comes on."

To Exorcise the Demon That Hates all That Processing and Communication: Bite your lip and do it anyway, again and again. Remind yourself that this is necessary maintenance to keep things running smoothly. If you never change the fluids in your car or get it a new oil filter, sooner or later it will run dry and something bad will happen. If you have a fancier, newer car with more gadgets (see my last statement about polyamory being a costly lifestyle!) or even just several cars, that's a whole lot more maintenance. You can look at it that way or perhaps compare it to eating right and seeing the doctor before your minor infection becomes life-threatening. It's just something that you have to do in order to keep everything running smoothly.

Besides, if things are quietly going wrong, it's better to know about them than to have them jump you from behind. Repeat to yourself, "Words are better than silence. Angry words are better than angry silence." Learn to not fear confrontation; part of the tricks that this demon uses is the image of all those people you care about being made upset because you brought up a sensitive subject, and it's all your fault, if only you'd left well enough alone . . . Counter-imagine everyone breaking up because you didn't say anything. Use this image to bolster yourself into taking the first deep breath and letting the words come out.

THE LESSER DEMONS

At every Polyamory 101 workshop or panel that I've been on, one of the first questions that comes up is: "How do you deal with jealousy?" I've always been uncomfortable with people who say breezily that "it just isn't a problem for me anymore, you just get over it" (which may be true for them, but isn't helpful to the people asking) or who suggest in subtle or not-so-subtle ways that jealousy is just a flaw that one ought to cast out. Telling someone that they shouldn't have whatever feelings they are having is never useful, and I've never seen it work in all the many years I've been processing feelings with people, which add up to quite a few. All it seems to do is to make the person feel bad about themselves and their unacceptable feelings, and keep quiet about them until things reach a head and explode. It's like putting summer tires on your car and telling the sky that it shouldn't be snowing, and then being angry when you skid into a guardrail. Instead, the group needs to deal with jealousy and its various accomplices as ordinary things that just happen and need to be worked out.

Having watched all the various green-eyed demons, I'd like to sort them out into piles, so that we can see them clearly and define their habits, feeding, and banishment. I've found that it makes sense to divide them into four species: jealousy, possessiveness, territoriality, and envy. I'd like to define these four demons as being slightly different and requiring different sorts of exorcism. It's true that in general practice, these four words are often used interchangeably, but I've found it useful to isolate them into specific emotional states, each with its own source and solution.

I. Jealousy

Jealousy, the most common demon to plague the practice of polyamory, is an emotional response based around low self-worth and insecurity. Its surface mask is simple fear of loss, but underneath is a deep and abiding feeling that whomever else your lover is attracted to will be better than you in some way. This demon whispers, "He (or she) doesn't really love you as much as they say they do. As soon as they find something better, they're going to dump you for that situation. And look at everything they have to choose from! That one's prettier than you. That one has thinner thighs. That one makes more money. That one is more charming, more charismatic. That one has kinkier, more exciting sex than you. That one's better at pretending to be 'sensitive.' That one is the gender that they've always fantasized about playing with. That one is manipulative, and your lover is dumb enough that they'll fall for that. How can you possibly measure up to all these other people, as inferior as you are? And how can you trust your lover not to want any of those options more than they want you? Wouldn't you, if you were them?"

Banishing this demon is a two-pronged approach. You have to do part of the job, and your lover has to do the other part. The first thing to do is to drag the nasty little sucker out onto the table where both of you can see it. That can be pretty embarrassing; no one likes to admit that they've been harboring a horrid little parasite, but the jealousy demon thrives in the dark and becomes weaker when exposed to light. Once it's out, your job is to work on your own self-esteem. Sometimes this can be as simple as repeating a list of affirmations about one's own worth, as a person and as a lover: "I am an attractive human being." "I am worthy of love." "I'm good at caring for another person." "My lover is lucky to have me in their life."

Of course, affirmations don't work for everyone, especially in the face of deeply rooted insecurities. Using affirmations is based on the "fake it till you feel it" principle, which can work wonders or not work at all, depending on the person in question and how invested they are in remaining unchanged. If this approach doesn't work for you, then you need to go out and do things that actually do work. Find activities that play on your strengths and make you feel confident and strong. Ask your partner to assist and support you in doing these things.

Your partner has a job to do as well. Their part in banishing this demon is to persist in trying to get you to believe that they really do love you and find you wonderful enough that they have no intention of leaving you. They need to say this again and again and do the things that drive it home. Karen in New England reminds us that "when someone gets jealous, it's because their needs aren't being met and they are insecure . . . so you have to give a little extra attention so that they know they are loved, and so very special."

You might try making it an ongoing dialogue: you say, "The demon is saying that you think he's sexier than me," and your partner says, "I think you're wonderfully sexy. Your eyes just melt my heart when you look at me that way, and you have sexy hands," and so forth. Try to make it into an affectionate exchange and not a desperate one; that way, it becomes a team effort against the demon, a loving collusion that brings the two of you closer. Of course, all compliments and special activities should be returned in kind.

To Exorcise the Jealousy Demon: On a piece of paper the color of sickly green, write every word the demon says to you. Phrase it in the second person: "You are _____." "You can't trust _____." "_____ is better than you in _____ way." Speak the statements aloud. Roll it up and tie it with sharp wire. If the ends stick you, so much the better. Acknowledge that pain.

On a piece of white paper, write the counter-answers to every one of those statements. Phrase them in the first person: "I am worthy of love." "I can trust my lover." "I am just as desirable as _____." Speak the statements aloud. Fold it up small and tie it with a small bit of soft ribbon.

Light a fire in a metal bowl or other fire-safe space with ventilation. Hold the green paper in one hand and the white paper in the other, and say, "You are not welcome in my mind." Take many deep breaths, inhaling deeply and exhaling completely. With each exhalation, blow through the tube of paper and visualize breathing out the voice that speaks these words. On each inhalation, hold the white packet to your heart and visualize breathing its words into you instead, spoken in a calm, accepting voice.

Drop the green paper into the fire, and say, "You are not welcome in my soul." Let it burn to ashes. Tuck the white paper into your clothing so that it rests next to your body. When the green paper is burned to ashes, collect the ashes and put them in a cup of water to drown, and say, "You are not welcome in my heart." Take the cup of water outside, dump it onto some patch of earth, and say, "You are not welcome in my life."

Sleep with the white paper under your pillow for as long as it takes. Carry it with you on your person. It's your shield. It's all right to open it and read it over again, as long as you retie it.

II. Possessiveness

This demon is similar to the demon jealousy, but there are subtle shades of difference to his motives, even if his footprints look similar. Those who are dogged by this demon tend to put a great deal of power into their possessions. As children, they were the ones who found it hard to share, because they couldn't trust that it was going to come back or that there would ever be enough. On some level, they are hoarders, stockpiling against a time of famine. One wonders if they spent many past lives in poverty and somehow got the need to have things in order to survive confused with the need to have love in order to survive. This emphasis on *having* rather than on experiencing makes them vulnerable to the possessiveness demon.

The voice of possessiveness has a somewhat different sound than that of jealousy. It whispers, "There isn't enough love in the world to go around. There's barely enough love for you to get your needs met. There's certainly not enough love—or attention, or time, or warmth, or sex—in your lover to nourish more than just you. If they go spreading it around elsewhere, there won't be enough for you. That's *your* love, *your* attention, *your* sex they're giving away. They promised it to you. It belongs to you. If you let them out of your sight, you'll lose it."

The opposite of possessiveness—and the state toward which someone beleaguered by this demon should be striving—is not an ascetic I-don't-need-anything-you-can-have-it-all situation, however attractive that might look to someone doing a martyr trip. The opposite of possessiveness is generosity, plain and simple. If you are being generous, it means that you have enough to share. You can give plenty away and still not be impoverished. It's that feeling of pure abundance when you know that you've got enough of whatever it is that you can give it out by the handfuls and still be knee-deep in it. The possessiveness demon doesn't go away by being told by the lover, "You don't own me, or my love, or my sex. You don't have me. I, and my love or sexuality, are not possessions to be *had*." While that may be true, the sort of person who is most plagued by this demon won't be helped by hearing this. More likely, their gut reaction will be, "Well, if I don't possess any part of you, then you might as well get out, because that's an emotional deal-breaker for me."

Instead, they need to learn to see *having* as a privilege that is paid for by *sharing*. To do this, they have to learn at a deep level that there is more than enough love, or attention, or warmth, or sex to go around. If they can be convinced that there's plenty, then sharing becomes a good thing. You give some of the extra that you possess to another, and they're made happy, and it's all good.

In many tribal societies, the chieftainship is based on the "big man" model of social capital—the idea being that the richer you are, the more obligated you are to throw big parties where those who have less get fed, thus spreading your wealth around rather than hoarding it. The man who throws the biggest parties is the chief, so long as he keeps giving back to the community in this way. By being generous, he creates a magic cycle of return whereby he keeps being given wealth by the universe, but if he gets greedy or scared that supplies will run out, he falls from grace, his wealth dries up, and he is deposed. The best way to deal with the possessiveness demon is to make a commitment to become that big man (or big woman) in your mind. You need to realize that whether or not this magic cycle works for things like money and physical resources (and personally, I believe that it does), it most certainly works this way for love. By being generous with your partner's favors, you make a deal with the universe that you will always have enough to keep you satisfied and to share. The "enough" may come in unusual ways that you didn't predict, but the gods are usually pretty good with that sort of thing.

Of course, if you're the partner of someone who is struggling to be generous with your favors, you can help them keep this mindset by making extra sure that you aren't actually shorting them. Nothing kills a generous mindset faster—and invokes the possessiveness demon quicker—than actually being robbed of agreed-upon privileges. Help your partner to articulate how much of you they need to feel satisfied, and keep that agreement. For example, if they need to see you four nights a week, and they need some kind of physical closeness on at least three of those nights, keep that schedule religiously. It helps if any other lovers that you have can actually bring themselves to say, "Thank you for your generosity in being so good about my seeing your partner."

To Exorcise the Possessiveness Demon: Ask your lover to bake a whole lot of heart-shaped cookies of your favorite flavor. If your lover can't bake, have them buy the cookies (or cakes, or whatever) at the bakery. If you don't like sweets, use some other sort of food. If possible, your lover should touch the food in question and visualize the feeling of their love flowing into it. Have your lover plop the whole lot in your lap, kiss you, and ceremonially say, "I love you. Help yourself. There's plenty." Eat until you are literally gorged. Keep saying to yourself, "There's more where that came from." When you can't eat any more, bring the rest to a party and give them away, or have people over to help you eat them. As you give them away, say, "I have enough to share and still be filled." This should be followed immediately by sending your lover off to some other romantic adventure, if one is planned.

III. Territoriality

Territoriality is entirely different. It's instinctive rather than emotional, coming out of the survival programming at the base of the brain. It's a special problem for alpha types of any gender, who seem to have a larger instinctive dose of it than non-alpha types. We don't like to acknowledge it, but we are descended from primates who lived in hierarchies with an alpha male and (usually) an alpha female as well. They marked their territory and defended it, and that included mates as well as land. For territorial types, this part of their deep brain is very strong, and it's linked to survival. To lose one's territory, the lizard-brain screams, is to lose all one's resources and starve to death.

Territoriality doesn't go away by increasing self-esteem. In fact, that can actually make it stronger, as the primitive alpha urges are increased by feelings of strength, as in "I'm so much stronger, of course I can better defend my territory now!" That doesn't mean that a person with a tendency toward territoriality should be kept down and demoralized for the safety of their lovers, but it does mean that there is no easy way out of the problem. Frankly, it's all up to the person with the urges to tame that beast.

To a certain extent, it helps to brainstorm possible ways of assuaging that territoriality with your lover—for example, it might be important for the territorial lover to do something physical immediately after their lover comes home from visiting another lover—but the problem is often that there's no such thing as "enough" for territorial types. This is a feeling that comes from the primitive animal inside us, and we have to face and deal with that animal on its own terms.

To Exorcise the Territoriality Demon: The territoriality demon isn't something that you necessarily want to cast out, because all too often it is part of our survival instinct and our will to live. Instead, you want it to realize that you are in charge, rather than it. This demon intimately and instinctively understands the hierarchy of the pack, and if you have it, so do you—even if you've been so steeped in nonhierarchical structures that you think you've left all that behind.

The first thing to do is to imagine this demon. See the animal that it is; acknowledge that it's an alpha in the pack or herd by nature. Appreciate its strength and power. Speak to it, and tell it that you are challenging it for the right to rule your life. Now visualize battling with it. It may help to actually jump on something like a pillow and wrestle and punch. If you can't win, you need to do some serious interpersonal work to figure out why. Ideally, you should force it to show its throat to you, or some other signal of submission. Inform it that you are now the one in charge, the alpha in this body, and that's just the way it is.

Once it has submitted to you, it is no longer your enemy. It is your dependent, and your responsibility is to feed it. You'll need to come up with things that make it feel appreciated, in exchange for no longer letting it have your lovers as its territory. For example, perhaps it wants a particular room for its den, and it would feel better if no one came in without knocking and asking permission. Perhaps it would like some carefully negotiated "rough play" with a friend or lover. Find out what your alpha demon wants and feed it, or it will get uppity again and need to be knocked back down.

IV. Envy

The demon that people don't generally expect to pop up is envy. This is one that can occur even when all parties are committed to polyamory and reasonably fine with letting their lovers have sexual relations with others. This is usually a particular problem when one partner finds it easier to attract new lovers than the other. It isn't always fair, but people judge harshly and often superficially when cruising for prospects, and if you are not attractive in a socially acceptable way, or you're shy, or have poor flirting/dating skills, or are male, it may be harder for you to find ready partners. The partner who can get lovers easily sometimes becomes a target of envy for the one who can't.

This plagued my first relationship far more than issues of jealousy, to my chagrin. My partner and I were clear from the start that this would be an "open relationship"—we didn't know the word "polyamory" at the time—and we granted each other veto power over prospective lovers. I went out and found another lover with surprising ease, but my partner was quieter, shyer, less sure of himself, fairly overweight, and inexperienced at dating (I had seduced him, and he'd never had to take the pursuer role). After a year, he had still not found a lover, and I'd gone through three of them. It became clear through his resentments that not only was he gratingly envious of my luck, he really wanted me to wait to find another lover until he had one himself, so that we could be "even." I felt bad for him—he felt like a kid watching other kids have fun with new toys while he had to make do with the same old ones—but there wasn't much I could do. I decided that I was not willing to wait until he got lucky, because that could be years for all I knew.

I also wasn't willing to find him a lover, which crops up sometimes for other people having envy problems. "My former boyfriend told me that if I wanted another boyfriend, I was going to have to provide him with a girlfriend," Brenna from Wisconsin grumbles. "For a while I tried looking for someone who might want to be with him, but in the end I felt like he wanted me to pimp for him, and I said no. We broke up soon after that."

Moira Wolf in Arizona speaks poignantly about her issues in this way: "Storm is not so much jealous *of* Nite as he is jealous *because of* Nite. What do I mean? He sees me and Nite together and wonders why he can't have that feeling with someone. Why can't he find a woman to be that close to, to have that passion with? What's wrong with him that no other woman wants him? He understands that I'm not going to get rid of him just because I also have Nite, but he's jealous of what we have that he doesn't. I wouldn't mind adding another woman for him, but he can't seem to find one who can accept us."

To Exorcise the Envy Demon: First, make a list of all the ways in which you and your partner are different. Roll up the list and tie it in a cord with four knots, saying the following:

> *I am on one path,*
>
> *And you are on another.*
>
> *Our paths may run together,*
>
> *But the lessons I face along the way are mine,*
>
> *As the lessons you face are yours.*

All I can do is help you to face yours,

All you can do is help me to face mine.

Next, make a list of those differences where you are better, or stronger, or luckier, or have more advantages in some way. If you can't think of any or your list is pitifully short, then either you're married to Superman or Mother Teresa, or you need to go out and work on your self-esteem, learn new skills or refine old ones, and in general try to get a life outside of your relationship. When you have a reasonable list, roll it up and tie it in a cord with four knots, saying the following:

I am on one path

And you are on another.

Our paths may run together,

But the gifts I receive are mine alone,

As the gifts you receive are yours alone.

All I can do is bask in your happiness,

All you can do is take joy in mine.

Now place the two rolls of paper over each other at right angles, so that they form a cross. Lash them in place with more string. Hang them up where they can be seen on a daily basis, and say the following:

I am on one path,

And you are on another,

But we live our lives together

At the crossroads of love.

The gods send you what is yours,

The gods send me what is mine.

I release you to receive your gifts and your lessons

Without judgment as to their worthiness.

I open myself to receive my gifts and lessons

And trust that the gods know best in this moment.

Whenever you feel envious, look up at the cross on the wall and repeat this last charm. It will get the attention of the gods, who will appreciate your efforts and give you what it is that you deserve.

Sun

Shiny New Lover Syndrome

"Make new friends but keep the old;
One is silver and the other's gold."

The sun is the biggest thing in the solar system, and the brightest, and the object with the most gravity. Everything else is held in check, revolving around it. Astrologically and magically, the sun symbolizes life-giving warmth, confidence, performance, and the self. The gods and goddesses of the sun are usually charismatic and important in any pantheon. The sun is a big deal, and it sometimes thinks of itself as an even bigger deal than it is. Arrogance is also a part of that solar energy.

One of the biggest pitfalls in any polyamorous relationship is the peculiar-to-poly disease that we refer to as Shiny New Lover Syndrome. In some parts of the poly demographic, people refer to "NRE," or New Relationship Energy. It's that feeling you get when you've just met someone new, and they're terrific and wonderful and, in some cases, everything your existing relationship is not. (This often happens because we tend to go looking, consciously or unconsciously, for new partners who "fill in the blanks" of qualities we don't currently have in our lovers.) In other words, NRE is a euphemism for that old demon, Falling In Love.

Having a new lover is a wonderful experience for everyone, and I'm certainly not putting it down or saying that you shouldn't enjoy it. However, if you are adding a new relationship to an old one, you have to be very, very careful. There's a line that you cross when NRE becomes Shiny New Lover Syndrome, and it isn't pretty . . . or rather, it may be beautiful to the two new lovebirds, but it isn't pretty to the existing partner(s) who's suffering through it.

When Shiny New Lover Syndrome strikes, it's as though the sun has lit up your entire life. The new partner, and the new relationship, become a brilliant light that shines on everything, giving it a golden glow and possibly blinding you to other things . . . like other pre-existing partners, who may seem dull and drab by comparison. The things that you do with them are new, too, and you want to do those exciting new things . . . a lot. It's easy for you to forget to spend enough time with your old partner(s) and even easier for you to feel grudging or distracted when you're reminded that you need to spend time with them. Even if you dutifully show up to your weekly tennis match or cuddling session, your mind may be elsewhere and, more to the point, your heart may also be elsewhere. YuleCat of Massachusetts ruefully admits: "It's been a while since I've had a good dose of New Relationship Energy, and my third partner and I are absolutely basking in it these days. As much as I love my other two partners, there's no way I can get NRE from either of them again. And that's okay."

And all too often, they can tell. Shiny New Lover Syndrome can generate huge arguments, demands, and conflicts. To the person on the other end, it feels suspiciously like you've left them, even when you're still there. It can create a kind of weird panic in them, which they may or may not be able to acknowledge. After all, if you'd actually left them for that person, it might be terrible and sad, but at least they'd be able to get on to the business of mourning the relationship and moving on. If you're still theoretically committed to them, still there in their lives as their lover, perhaps still sleeping in bed with them at night and waking up with them in the morning, they can't exactly say that you've left. They may figure out, though, that your attention isn't with them any more, that the light in your eyes looks past them now.

If they are consciously trying to practice polyamory ethically, they may feel as though they can't fairly accuse you of doing anything wrong, so to speak. They may push aside their feelings of resentment and abandonment, put a brave face on it, and try to be grateful that at least you're still around. On the other hand, they may start demanding more and more of your attention, even if (and perhaps especially if) it cuts into your time with the Shiny New Lover. One can imagine the kind of conflict that this can engender. One woman who was feeling left out by her husband and his new lover would periodically walk into the bedroom when they were having sex and start loud monologues on random subjects as a way of communicating her frustration.

The first step to dealing with this issue is, of course, honest communication about the situation. It can also be true that for an insecure prior lover, the fear of abandonment can be so strong that they may suspect Shiny New Lover Syndrome even when it isn't present. Arguing over whether one is actually suffering from this malady is often an exercise in futility. After all, if you're in the middle of it, you might not realize that you're doing it, especially if you're not the introspective type; similarly, telling the insecure partner that you don't feel that way may not be believable to them. It's better to start by asking whether there is anything that you can do to make them feel more secure about your love for them, and start from there.

When a new lover enters an established relationship—especially if they are only lovers with, or only emotionally close with, one member of the relationship; especially if the people involved are new to polyamory; especially if it's the first new addition in a long time—there can be an almost instant bout of insecurity to deal with. One of the hardest things that anyone can do is to admit to their lover that they feel insecure, even when they aren't assuming that they will be abandoned. Another of the hardest things that anyone can do is to just sit quietly, listen to what is being said, and ask one's self as objectively as possible whether one's own actions contributed to the problem. People tend to react instead by getting defensive, and as soon as you do that, the insecure partner is the Enemy, and trust has been further breached.

I'll get to dealing with issues of trust in Jupiter's chapter. For the moment, let's just say that Shiny New Lover Syndrome (SNLS) is like a drug, and if you don't want to be pushed into kicking it entirely by a breakup, you'd better learn how to manage it effectively. The irony, which I can attest to by both observation and experience, is that when people break up from SNLS, they tend to do it more than once. In other words, if Jane has a habit of succumbing to SNLS, and she lets her new feelings for Bob break her up with Joe, the likelihood is that somewhere down the road she'll let her feelings for Sam break her up with Bob.

If you're the new lover coming into this situation, you'd better keep that in mind. The gods are fair that way, and the Law of Return counts. Watch how your new poly lover treats his or her existing relationships very carefully, because no matter how cute or interesting you are, sooner or later you'll be the established lover (or one of them), and someone new might come along, and it'll be your turn in the barrel. If they do it to one partner, they'll do it to another, unless they recognize their pattern and stop. And if you contribute to the problem or are complicit with their poor treatment of their current partner, the Law of Return will make certain that you will eventually be similarly served, if only because you *will* be in their place someday if you stay with this person and no changes are made.

Ceasing SNLS can often be harder than it looks, though. Our culture pushes the falling-in-love soulmate fantasy pretty hard, and it gets programmed early into our brains. That archetype contains the idea that it is impossible to love two people at once. We're never taught how to do that, except perhaps with our parents, and that's a different situation because they're not our equals, and their most important relationship (which we are never allowed inside) is with each other and not us. To love two equals simultaneously is subtly discouraged in our society. We're asked which friend is our best friend, not which are our three best friends. It's assumed that in any group of people, we'll like one more than any of the others, and that ranking is just part of the way things are done. Parents are supposed to love all their children equally, but there's often an accepted assumption that one child is the favorite, or perhaps one kid is Mom's kid and one kid is Dad's kid, or something like that. And, of course, you're supposed to have one lover that you love more than anyone else. Sometimes loving more than one person at a time is a skill that must be learned the hard way.

There are two ways to come at this problem. You can scale back on your overwhelmingly idealistic feelings for the new person, or you can concentrate on bringing the passion back into your original relationship, or you can do both.

The first one is the harder path, because it feels so awful. We all have a tendency to idealize the people we're in love with, and that golden halo is just so beautiful that we can't bear to rip it off them. We aren't suggesting that you try to fall out of love with your new lover, but sometimes part of the reason that you may be wanting to spend so much time with them has more to do with your idealized image of them (and how superior they are to your current lover) than with the actual reality of their personality. Deliberately concentrate on things you don't like about them. Throw yourself into situations that stress those uncomfortable points. If you're nervous about your new lover going to strip clubs and jeering at naked girls, go with him, watch him do it, and see if it still bothers you. If it's really going to last for any serious length of time, you'd have to deal with these things anyway, so it's best to get on with it. If tarnishing that halo ruins the relationship, well, it wouldn't have made it anyway.

Self-Binding Spell to Combat SNLS

This spell should only be taken on with a whole heart. In other words, no one should be pressured into doing it by a resentful lover. Do it only if it seems to be the absolute most right thing to do, because if much of your subconscious rebels against a spell that you lay on yourself, the spell may be sabotaged by those parts of you. Ideally, you should let all your lovers know that you're doing it, whether they approve or not.

You will need a stone carved into a heart, any size. What sort of stone it is will vary with the person involved. The best thing is to pick up heart-shaped stones and hold them to your heart chakra; some will resonate more than others. The idea is to find one that best symbolizes your own emotional processes. For some, that will be a "traditional" heart chakra stone like rose quartz; for others, it will be something more nontraditional.

You will also need a cord of a color that symbolizes commitment to you. Some people have chosen white, as it's the wedding color in our culture, especially when the existing relationship is an actual post-wedding marriage. Others have used black, the color of Saturn and bindings. Still others have used red for honor, or blue for reason, or green for the endurance of the earth. It should be geared to the size of your stone heart; if it's a tiny, locket-sized pendant, a colored thread will do. You will also need a quiet place, an uninterrupted period of time, and some kind of light source—a candle, a lantern, even a light bulb.

Create sacred space for yourself, however you do that, whether it's calling the quarters or casting a circle in some other way or just sitting quietly and meditating until you feel safe and grounded. Do not do this ritual in a dark place; it should be well lit. There should be nothing shadowy or secret about this rite; it is an act of bringing things into the light and scrutinizing them. Hold the heart up to the light so that it is haloed in the glow, and force yourself to stare at it without blinking until you reach the point of discomfort. As you do so, say these words:

> *The sun lights up the sky,*
>
> *And my heart glows with the light of a new sun,*
>
> *And her (his) name is _____ (name of new lover).*
>
> *But I know that if the sun is left*
>
> *To burn all things unchecked,*
>
> *Its life-giving rays will turn to death-dealing,*
>
> *And tender things will wither and die in its light,*
>
> *And leave a desert behind.*
>
> *I do not wish the love I have for _____ (name of existing lover)*
>
> *To wither away to nothing,*
>
> *Or to burn up in fires of resentment,*
>
> *So I do hereby bind my heart*
>
> *Of my own free will,*
>
> *As the atmosphere gently binds Earth*
>
> *In many turns of the winds,*
>
> *And gives it protection.*
>
> *My love for _____ (name of new lover) will still be*
>
> *   just as strong,*
>
> *But it will not overtake my life*
>
> *So violently that all other loves*
>
> *Will be consumed in its flame.*
>
> *I have spoken; so mote it be.*

Repeat the last line nine times. As you say each repetition, wind the string once around the stone heart and knot it. After nine turns and nine knots, hold it again to your heart. You should carry it there, perhaps in a bag around your neck, or a pocket—one person fastened it there for a while with a piece of medical tape—for at least a few hours. When you remove it, put it in a safe place where it won't be lost or bothered. If at some point you feel that it has done its job and is no longer necessary, carefully cut the bonds with a sharp knife, burn them in a fire of some sort, and return the stone to its safe place.

Spell to Rekindle the Flame of Love

The second path is somewhat easier, if slower and requiring more attention. This is a matter of rekindling the flame of the old love in such a way that it is able to "compete" with the attraction of the newer one. This, too, must be done with a whole heart and preferably with a sense of enthusiasm.

Start by making a list of all the various things that you love about your existing lover. If you're coming up short, it may be that your relationship was honestly in trouble before the Shiny New Lover came into the picture, and in fact your bad case of SNLS may well be a symptom of repressed resentments or disappointments stemming from undealt-with issues. You probably should have been dealing with these issues all along, but it's too late for regretting that now. However, you can start working on the relationship honestly right now, even if that means drastic measures like couples' therapy or mediation.

I'm assuming, though, that you took up with this person because you loved them, you were attracted to their good qualities, and you still think that this relationship is good and worth fighting for. So write that list of good qualities, roll it up, and stick it under your pillow. Sleep that way for a minimum of three nights (which you should spend in bed with them, by the way). After at least three nights (but not too much more than that), find a large pillar-type candle of a color that corresponds to the part of your relationship that most needs rekindling. If it's gone sexually south, get a red one; if what you need is more affection, try a pink one; for general solidity and trust, try green. Carve the rune Gyfu on it (for those of you who don't know runes, it looks like a *X* and symbolizes crossroads and partnership), or a heart, or the symbol for Venus (♀), or a word like *Love* or *Desire*, or all of the above. Then carve their name above those symbols. Get up early in the morning, as the sun is rising. Sit in a quiet place where you can see the sunrise; hold the list, and read it once more. Say the following:

> *Fire is warmth and light,*
>
> *Fire is safety and protection,*
>
> *Fire is a beacon in the darkness,*
>
> *Fire is nourishment made together,*
>
> *Fire is a place for song and story,*
>
> *Fire is what makes a house a home.*
>
> *Our fire has waned as we slept,*
>
> *As every fire dies to coals during the night,*
>
> *But it is morning now, and we will rise,*
>
> *And we will feed those coals and embers,*
>
> *So carefully and lovingly kept,*
>
> *And our fire will rise again*
>
> *To burn strong and hot until night falls once more,*
>
> *And should it burn again to embers,*
>
> *We will have faith that this miracle*
>
> *Can be worked again and again.*

I want this flame of love with all my heart,

And this is my will,

So mote it be.

Light the candle and set it in a place where it can burn down. It is not a terrible omen if it burns out before it's consumed—there are always winds and drafts and pooling wax—but ideally it should go for a significant amount of time. Then follow this up immediately by doing some activity with your first lover, preferably something that you both love to do and have traditionally done together.

As the days pass, actively work on spending time with them and concentrating on their good qualities. If you think that the problem is your own inability to love more than one person intensely, maybe you ought to talk to the Love Goddess about that and get her advice.

Mars

Honorable Opponents

In astrology, Mars is that planet of action, passion, anger, and will. It is the internal warrior who fights for the goal and for your own defense. Mythically, Mars was the Roman god of war and the protector of cities. He was a fiery god, as Mars is astrologically a fiery planet, and everything that he did, he did with a bang.

When we start relationships, we often go into them with the secret (or not so secret) illusion that this relationship will be the best one, the perfect one, and "perfect" often means "no conflict" to us. Of course, it's impossible. Every relationship has conflict sooner or later, and when there will be several people for whom it is imperative to get along, work should be put into learning how to manage it effectively.

Effective conflict does not mean that all arguments must be conducted in level, dispassionate voices that never get loud or angry. It does mean that all fighting take place face to face, at least metaphorically: no backstabbing, no use of deliberately hurtful or derogatory terms, and no remarks that are merely designed to make others look stupid. That's hard to do when your ire is up and adrenaline is rampaging through your system. Some people are so afraid of their inability to fight effectively that they prefer never to fight at all, but that means they either get perennially run over or they finally explode and flail around, doing a lot of destruction but not getting anything done.

It would take more than this meager chapter in this one book to learn how to fight effectively in relationships, but the first step is simple and straightforward: accept that fighting is both inevitable and necessary. Accept that with all your heart. There are just as many gods of war as there are gods of love, and sometimes they are bedfellows . . . or the same entity. Conflict is as integral to any path of human interaction as harmony. In fact, real harmony is impossible if underlying conflicts are being ignored. Honorable fighting clears the air and allows true peace in the end. Remember that in Greek mythology, the demigoddess Harmonia is the daughter of Aphrodite and Ares—Love and War. Why is this coupling important? Because Mars is passion as well as anger. Without any acknowledgment of anger, without any honest conflict, relationships become passionless and cold. The will to stay together seems to slowly dissolve. In order to keep things warm, you have to risk explosions. You don't throw out your furnace and shiver in the cold because sometimes furnaces explode. You keep it well maintained and well stoked, and you check it often. You acknowledge the danger, and you work to make it safer without putting out the flame.

The Tashlins, a triad in Massachusetts, comment: "One thing that is not talked about is the potential for true havoc when a poly family fights. This may be more difficult for us because we are always working not to have a hierarchical structure. This sometimes just ends up being a fluid hierarchy, and the pecking order is different for different areas of life . . . Our arguing situation is further complicated by the fact that Storm grew up in a family which handled conflict very differently than Fire's or Winter's family, who are more directly verbally confrontational. Storm's family avoided any subjects which couldn't be discussed calmly and rationally, even to the extent of avoiding any emotionally charged topics at all. This has led to a great deal of compromise; especially when the argument is only between two parties, we have found it important to avoid having two members gang up on the third. This includes necessary limitations on things like grip-ing about one partner to the other out of earshot or having a partner venture an unasked-for opinion on a disagreement between the other two. However, we try to remember that we are people with human feelings and that sometimes it is okay to simply be pissed off. Storm has had to learn that just because people yell at each other doesn't mean they don't love each other or are breaking up."

The second step is to declare the value and importance of being an honorable warrior. This includes actually having a code of behav-ior that places limits on how you will behave when your back is against the wall. It's easy to hold to a code of honor when every-thing's going well, but when you're furious and/or terrified, it gets a lot harder. That's when you figure out whether you actually believe in this code of honor or whether it's a decoration that gets tossed as soon as the excrement hits the fan. Fighting with your loved ones can feel like your own psychic survival is threatened, and it's at that moment of adrenaline-laced, primitive fight-or-flight that the inner warrior either keeps the strength to hold to his rules, or he loses it and becomes a mindless berserker, slashing randomly at whatever seems to be the enemy to his befuddled mind.

Start by putting your code of honor down on paper. It doesn't have to be fancy; it can say things simply, like "I will not call my lovers insulting names during fights," or "I will not make insulting suggestions to my lovers when I am angry at them," or "I will not say things that I know are not true just because I am angry." If you feel the need to remind yourself that physical violence toward another person is always unacceptable, then that should be put at the top of the list.

If possible, everyone involved in the relationship should also do this exercise, and then the codes can be posted and discussed. At no time should anyone tell anyone else that anything on their list is wrong, or missing, or otherwise unacceptable. The discussion should only work around how all these different but perfectly serviceable codes of honor might clash with each other and how to prevent that and do damage control when it happens.

The third step in polyamorous fighting is the old Pagan understanding that words have power. Part of this is, of course, that words coming from people who are important to your life have a strong impact on you emotionally, and untrue cruel words said only for the sake of venting feelings can permanently damage someone's trust in you as a reasonable human being. If you're prone to saying things that you don't mean and then apologizing afterwards—"I didn't really mean it, I was just angry/hurt/resentful, and therefore you should excuse what I said"—it would be in your best interest to learn to get beyond that behavior. You're practically asking for your lovers to disbelieve anything you you say in the heat of the moment, and it's likely that in practice this will not only make you angrier but destroy their trust in you and your ability to be honest. Although courtesy may seem stilted in arguments with lovers, it's sometimes better to err on the side of stilted than out of control.

Oberon Zell-Ravenheart points out that "the guides to treating a polyamorous partner well are the same basic principles of civility that apply to any human interaction. One may have to adhere to them more strictly and consciously in polyamory, and mistakes may have more dramatic outcomes. The game of human civility has higher stakes when more people are involved intimately."

Words have power on another level as well. In general, relationships tend to follow archetypal paths. Sometimes those archetypes are well known to us, and sometimes they are ones that have been lost or have not yet been written down in this world. When you announce something about your relationship that has heretofore not been said, especially if you do it with intent, you can change the nature of the archetype. Sometimes this can be a very good thing, as when someone points out unspoken resentments or hidden agendas or assumptions that ought to be challenged. Sometimes it can have negative effects, because one person is redefining the relationship in a way that cannot help but affect everyone else involved. These statements can make "marks on the universe," so to speak, that may take a lot of work to clean up.

For example, let's take three people who are in a triad relationship. Two have a lot in common with regard to mental processes and discussion styles. The third has a different style of thinking and talking, which means that when arguments ensue, the first two partners tend to be more "in sync" with each other and understand each other's language better. This means that a lot more time gets spent on interpreting the third partner's wants and needs. The third partner is not unaware that she seems to be "at odds" with her partners for longer periods in arguments than they are with each other, and this leads to some resentment on her part. One day, in a fit of frustration, she cries out, "You two are always teaming up against me!"

Of course, the reflexive response of her other two partners is likely to be to jump to reassure her that of course they aren't always teaming up against her. However, her words have created an image in the atmosphere that they are a "team," and she is not on that team. If they rush to reassure her together, nothing they say will work because they'll still be acting like a team as far as she's concerned. In order to make the situation work, they will need to react against the image she's created, not just the truth or untruth of her words. If her image, thrown into the air between them, says that they are teaming up against her, then in order to fight that they need to separate for the moment and create separate reactions. They might also think of times when they'd been on her side against the other partner in some argument and call that image, mentally or verbally, in order to combat her vision.

In this particular case, if nothing is consciously done to combat the archetypal image that the third partner has called up, it will just get called up again and again and slowly mold and change the relationship until, indeed, the other two partners are spending most of their time as a "team," colluding on how to deal with their third lover. Of course, one must remember that every single person in a poly relationship has that same power of magically defining the situation, and they should use it . . . with caution and forethought for the power of their words.

There can be a lot of pressure in a polyamorous relationship to "make it work at all costs." Your friends may be watching you critically, just waiting for you all to break up so that they can start in with a chorus of "I told you so." Your own belief that polyamory can work, or the beliefs of your partners, may be hanging in the balance. It's not hard to slip into the pattern of downplaying conflict, especially where anyone else might notice, in order to keep embodying the "perfect poly relationship." Someone who is currently actively poly may feel more pressure than someone who doesn't have any other lovers at the moment, especially in a first-time poly situation.

Probably the most pressure is felt by someone who is at the point of a V-type relationship. Moira Wolf in Arizona explains that "if there's conflict, I take the brunt of it, because I don't want them fighting. If one has a complaint about the other, I'm the mediator. We rarely sit down and talk as a family, but we do when there are big decisions to be made, like buying a new house. But if there's conflict, I go from one to the other, and I take the anger. I look on this as the price I pay for the gift of polyamory. I want to be in the middle between my lovers, and I can't wiggle out when the middle happens to be the hot seat."

This system can work well if the person in the middle is a reasonably good mediator and if there is no serious ongoing animosity between their lovers. The problem becomes when the middle person actively interferes with direct interfacing between the two lovers in question, insisting that all communications must go through them.

It's not good for two people who are involved in the same complex emotional situation never to speak to each other. Even if there is a great deal of anger and dislike, they ought to be able to interact civilly when necessary.

If you're the centerpoint of a V and you've taken on the job of being mediator, remember that your eventual goal—even if it's never reached in your lifetime—should be getting everyone to the point where they are comfortable enough to speak to each other courteously with useful results, even when you're not there. I've seen situations where everything seems fine as long as the central person is always there to run back and forth and alleviate potential conflict, but as soon as that central person was ill and in the hospital, terrible fighting erupted among their various lovers. Make sure that your mediation doesn't make people too comfortable with never having to communicate directly.

If things get serious, what I often end up doing is making an offering to one of the love goddesses and asking their help in resolving the situation. Remember, one of the good things about being Pagan—and especially about being a polytheist—is that you have a number of deities to call on for help. It's all right to ask for help, especially if you're at the end of your rope with arguments. Propitiating the love goddesses to help is one option. I use a pink candle, sweet wine, and candy. After you do this ritual, be prepared to be open and cooperative with any reconciliatory moves your partners make.

If you really feel that you are wronged, make an offering to one of the goddesses of justice—Ma'at, for example, or Dike. The traditional offering is a feather, a blade, and a libation of clear water. Of course, a justice request will also rebound on you automatically, as it is only just that what you ask of another, you should put up with yourself. The better you bear your own injustices coming home to roost and learn to make up for them, the more the goddesses of justice will smile on you.

Another good spell is one to cool down anger. Sometimes, after a long period of problems, people can just get into the habit of being generally peeved and hostile. This spell is best done with everyone involved, and it should never be done behind someone's back. (It goes without saying that part of spiritual polyamorous ethics is that you never lay a spell on a lover without their prior knowledge, yes? Well, it should. Treat magical workings and outside sex with the same rules.) Put everyone's name on a small piece of paper, along with a cartoon face of them being enraged. Put them into a cup and pour cold water on them, saying, "Cool down, fiery heads." This is then put into the freezer. Remove the cup in one turn of the moon, let it melt, and have a discussion immediately afterward to test the tone of the household mood.

Mars Ritual for Honorable Fighting

In his book *Iron John*, the poet Robert Bly makes a gem of a comment about fighting as a couple: he suggests that each domestic warrior should identify their weapons. This is the follow-up to enumerating one's code of honor. Think about the weapons that you use. Are they honorable weapons, like the blade of reason, the hammer of honesty, or the shield of courtesy? Are they sneaky weapons, like the hidden bullet of insult, the stiletto of character assassination, the broadsword of great sweeping generalities, or the doorway lance (which is pulled out after the fight is ostensibly over and one person is going out the door, at which point the other one nails them to the doorframe with one last nasty comment)? Ask your partners which you tend to use. Ask your friends, at least the ones that you've argued with or who have seen you arguing. If it's generally agreed that your fighting style tends to become dishonorable under pressure, then you need to work on that. Start with this prayer:

PRAYER FOR A RELUCTANT WARRIOR

I stand before the east and call for your aid,

Athena of the olive branch,

Strategist and armored one,

Wise goddess of many shapes.

I ask for clarity of mind

In the face of the smoke that rises

From my smoldering heart.

I ask for clarity of words

In the face of the rage that rises

Like a dragon in my throat.

I beg for the understanding

Of the mind of my opponent,

That we may find the best road to peace.

I stand before the south and reach for your aid,

Durga of the tiger,

Destroyer of illusions,

Slayer of the demons of fear.

I ask for courage of the soul

To face my own illusions honestly

Through the weeping of my own wounds.

I ask for courage of the heart

To willingly enter in fair battle with my loved ones

And speak forth with no fear of retribution.

I beg to learn to believe in my opponent,

Who is also my lover,

That we may find the best road to mutual trust.

I stand before the west and call your name,

Brigid of the holy well,

Warrior of the sacred flame,

Healer, smith, maker of alphabets.

I ask for depth of feeling

That may be communicated with every word

In the face of the different languages of our souls.

I ask for depth of compassion,

That I may never forget

It is no monster who stands before me.

I beg for the conviction

That our connection serves our paths,

That we may find the best road to each others' hearts.

I stand before the north and call your name,

Thor, Lord of Thunder,

Straightforward Lord of Senses,

Son of the earth and sky.

I ask for the strength of hope

To keep going, step after step,

Even when all seems bleak between us.

I ask for the strength of honor,

Hard as the bedrock beneath us,

That I may never give in to pettiness.

I beg you to make my heart constant enough

To endure every blow without shattering,

That we may find the best road back home.

This should be said not together, but separately, preferably in separate spaces by those who are about to come together and do battle with each other. Then you should come together and announce your intentions clearly. This can be as simple as saying, "I want us to talk about Problem X. I'm willing to stick it out until we resolve something or we both decide that it can't be resolved. I have great faith that we can work this out."

Or, if you prefer something more ritual in tone, you can use this ritual challenge:

CHALLENGE FOR THE BELOVED IN BATTLE

I come before you armed

But not vicious in my attack;

I will strike only honorable blows.

I come before you shielded

But not invulnerable to you;

I love you and my heart is open.

I come before you with only hope in my heart

And only truth on my lips.

I will say what I mean

And mean what I say.

Will you return this challenge?

Although these words may seem silly and stilted, by having each person involved speak them, it creates sacred space in which people are more reluctant to say or do deliberately malicious or petty things. It also creates a space where the gods are listening to your argument, and they will hold you to your word. That doesn't mean that you can't lie, or hit below the belt, or generally act like a jerk, but it means that what you do will come back to you quicker and more efficiently.

Wrongdoing in ritual space has severer consequences than wrongdoing in everyday life between the eggs and the bacon, but this should be the opposite of frightening or uncomfortable to the honorable warrior.

Jupiter
Trust and Honesty

Except that there is no perfect love and perfect trust, because we are human beings, and we aren't perfect. The only such thing is the love of the gods. We mortals don't come nearly so easily to love. It's a lot of work, and we don't like that at all, so we get it wrong again and again. We're even worse when it comes to trust. These things, unfortunately, are not taught to us in school. We have to learn them the hard way, and some of us never learn them properly at all. Some of us may be damaged in some way that makes it especially difficult for us to trust, and without real trust there can't be any real love.

Jupiter is the biggest planet in the solar system. In astrology, it symbolizes abundance, generosity, luck, good fortune, and a sort of state of grace where you trust the universe to take care of you, and it does. Where Jupiter is placed in your astrological chart, things come easily. You don't have to work or fight for them; they just seem to fall into your lap. There's always enough and more of anything that you need or want. When you live in Jupiter's world, even for a few minutes, you can afford to be generous.

For most of us, this situation does not seem to describe our love lives. In fact, most of us have a terrible time being generous with our romantic and sexual relationships. We are taught, in this culture, to have a scarcity consciousness about love. There's never enough of it, and the little bit of it that you get might be snatched away—or walk out on its own two feet—at any moment. We cling to it with everything we've got and snarl at possible poachers like a skinny predator defending a sparse and arid piece of land that is its bare survival. We don't know how to be generous because we really believe, down underneath, that not only do we not have enough now, but we've never had enough before, and we never will. And every time we break up with a lover it only confirms our belief in this idea.

Of course, it is also true that low self-esteem is practically the psychological common cold in our Western culture as well, so perhaps it isn't too surprising. Even if an existing couple is completely committed to polyamory, they may still have fits of irrational jealousy, possessiveness, territoriality, and envy—the fiery four that we discussed in the Fire chapter. Moira Wolf in Arizona says of her two lovers, "It hasn't been easy. Storm has had to learn not to be jealous, that I'm not going anywhere . . . he's had to accept my having someone else who I love also. Nite's had to learn to live with others and to not be afraid—isn't a wife's lover usually shot?"

Trust starts with honesty. It's as simple as that, although it doesn't end there. YuleCat in Massachusetts states bluntly: "I have a policy of brutal honesty with my lovers. Having lied about relationships in the past, I'm more inclined to tell everything at this point, even if the truth hurts, although I do try to be as gentle as I can." Trust cannot survive in an atmosphere of dishonesty; it can limp along blindly for a while, but sooner or later the depth of unsaid truths will emerge. It's better to be up-front about even your irrational and unacceptable feelings, because when they're shoved into the basement they tend to saw through the floor and make trouble.

One speaker on a panel about polyamory said it well: your established lover will hold up hoops for you to jump through in order to prove that you still love them, and you'd better get to jumping. It does no good to tell them that their hoops are unfair or a sign of mistrust. If there is mistrust or insecurity, you don't make it go away by telling them that they shouldn't have it. In fact, that will almost always make things worse. You make it go away by jumping through all the hoops, carefully and not grudgingly, and complaining about them as little as possible. If you really love them, then yes, you'll do these hoops. If they really love you, they'll see your effort and acknowledge it, and it will—eventually—assuage their fears.

When my boyfriend moved in with me and my wife, we hadn't had a live-in lover in a long time. It was also a formerly long-distance situation where I would travel six hours to spend the weekend with him, and it would end up being a vacation for both of us. She was rightfully worried that we would spend all our time acting like we were still on vacation, even though we now had to settle down and divide up household chores, so she held up a hoop: that we each take on bigger choreloads than her for a while. She needed us to prove to her that this move was a good thing, an addition of hands to help rather than a drain on the attention to household work. On the surface, this might have seemed unfair or spiteful; in our experienced poly household, the communication was good enough that we were able to read it as a hoop to be jumped through, a quest to be fulfilled, rather than a punishment to be endured.

Sometimes it helps to imagine this as the quest in the fairy tale, where the protagonist is set a series of difficult tasks, after which they will receive some precious thing. Often, the tasks seem to be designed around areas in which they are weak and need to improve themselves. If they give up, or shirk things, or attempt to cheat or cut corners, something always goes wrong, and they lose their chance and perhaps have to beg for another one. If you really love your existing partner, their trust is a precious jewel worth questing for.

On the other hand, if the quest is ripping you to pieces emotionally, if the place your partner needs you to go is so much further than your comfort zone that you begin to feel desperate, you may need to assert your own needs and ask for a compromise. It's also a problem when what you are asked to do compromises your integrity, asking you to become someone or something that you are not and cannot ever hope to be. There's no point in completing the quest if, by the time you reach the treasure, it just doesn't seem worth all the effort anymore.

YuleCat tells this story: "Back when A and I were unmarried, she became interested in a guy who I'll call E. A is bisexual, and emotionally, I have a bit of a double standard still. I'm completely okay with A doing whatever she wants to with women, but I have a bit more of a problem with her seeing other guys. I think it's a case of 'What does this person have that I don't?' In the case of a woman, it's obvious; for a guy, it's less so. However, I'm aware that this is an irrational thing, and I felt that it was an unfair double standard for me to have. It was also the first guy she'd been with since we'd been together. So I felt pressured—not by A, but by myself—to walk the walk if I'm going to talk the talk. And, on top of all this, A and E met when I had just lost my job, and my former employer was screwing me out of unemployment benefits, forcing A and I to survive on her minimal retail store wages alone. So the overall stress level in my life was already sky-high, without the additional melodrama. But rather than be honest with A, I squelched my emotions and told her to go ahead with E. I genuinely liked him as a person, but all these factors piled up were too much for me. I couldn't handle it, yet I didn't feel that my concerns were important enough to ask A to back off. Now I realize I shouldn't have done it. My excessive stress about the job situation was in itself a good enough reason to ask A to put the affair on hold."

He also relates what he's learned: "From that point on, I've been honest with A as to how I feel about the men she's interested in, and how comfortable I am with various stages of the relationship and the sexual relations. Rather than ignore my emotions because they don't make sense, we both listen to them and we both accept them, even if it is an unfair double standard. So if I'm not comfortable with the idea of A sleeping with a new male partner of hers, I tell her, and she won't do it—no questions asked. Similarly, now that I understand that my discomfort is strictly an irrational emotional response, I've learned how to deal with it. Basically, I get to know the guy myself, and as I get to know him, he ceases to be a threat in my mind and becomes a person. A's current male partner and I are good friends, and by addressing my irrational fears instead of ignoring them, I'm completely fine with their relationship."

This tale shows how important it is that people learn to identify and own their particular insecurities and triggers. Sandbagging—letting resentment pile up until it explodes—is guaranteed to kill a polyamorous relationship. The next step, of course, is figuring out something that your lover can do that will actually make a difference in that way. Coming to the table with a possible solution—or even several possible solutions that your lover can choose between—is more likely to get you an actual result instead of just hours of arguing.

I recently counseled a woman whose boyfriend was pressing for polyamory, and she was trying to decide whether or not it felt right. She couldn't help being insecure about him running off with other people; I pointed out that he still had not finished the legal paperwork on his last divorce and was being evasive about actually marrying her. I suggested that maybe polyamory might look a good deal different once he'd actually made a real commitment to her. In this case, there was a distinct possibility that her trust issues weren't unfounded personal neuroses at all and that she was perfectly reasonable in holding up the "hoop" of a solid commitment before leaping into polyamory.

Sometimes the problem is just that there's no way to get around the partner's deeply felt lack of trust. Some individuals are so damaged, often by brutal violations of their trust during childhood, that their lack of trust is almost pathological. You could stand on your head for weeks and it wouldn't help. In fact, nothing you can do will help them, because they have lost their ability to believe in something. People with pathological mistrust need help that you, their lover, can't give them. If you sense that your lover is one of these, you need to make the hard decision whether to remain with them and not be polyamorous or leave them.

While a partner with pathological mistrust issues can be a problem in any relationship, regardless of sexual and romantic arrangements, they become a poly problem most seriously when both people have agreed to be polyamorous, are now acting on the agreement, and suddenly there's nothing that one person can do to make their lover anything but unhappy with the new situation. This is a special problem when it sets up a double standard—"I can have other lovers, because I know you trust me, but you can't, because I can't trust you." If you really want to stay with such an individual, counseling is in order. To find out if this is really the problem, I suggest some rounds of divination.

Please don't mistake a lover who is merely quite monogamous by preference, and would prefer that you be monogamous too, for someone with pathological mistrust issues. If you're in that situation, you have to make the same decision, but it doesn't matter whether they have trust issues. For some monogamous people, exclusive sexual rights are an important way of showing love, one whose absence is a deal-breaker for them. When you ask them to let you be non-exclusive, it's not that you're asking them to trust you, it's that you're asking them to do without. All the trust in the world doesn't help if someone is not getting a deeply held emotional need met. I've seen the occasional rare relationship work between a poly person and a monogamous person, but only when the monogamous person did not see sexual exclusivity as the coin in which love was paid. Sometimes a monogamous person will try to be polyamorous in order to please their lover, and then they may discover that they can't adjust emotionally. This isn't about trust, it's about knowing one's needs and standing one's ground.

This chapter, under the reign of Jupiter, seems to be a good place to talk about a term that has sprung up in the polyamory community: *compersion*. This term refers to an emotional state where your insecurities are so low, your trust so high, and your value in the happiness of your partner(s) so far beyond your own baggage, that seeing them having good relationships with other lovers inspires nothing but joy and contentment in you. It's been described as "the state of knowing that your lover is getting it on noisily and happily with their lover on the other side of the wall, and feeling incredible satisfaction in knowing that." Compersion is the opposite of all the Greater Demons listed in the Fire chapter.

Compersion is one of the ideal end results of incorporating polyamory into one's spiritual practice. For people who attempt to practice polyamory as a spiritual path it is the ultimate emotional goal, just as unconditional appreciation of diversity is the ultimate goal for people who want to change the world. We may never fully achieve total compersion, but that doesn't mean that we shouldn't strive for it. That's an uncomfortable truth, and one that even experienced polyamorists don't like to examine closely, but it's true. There are many virtues that we should strive to reach, and just because we can't do it all today doesn't mean that we shouldn't try.

A friend of mine, who was a counselor, had a message on her answering machine that ended, "And remember: progress, not perfection." I used to call her house when I knew she wasn't home just so I could hear those words. That's kind of how I feel about compersion. I'd like to think that I learn a little more about trusting people, starting with the people that I love most, whenever I hold my breath, cross my fingers, and leap into trusting my lovers. So far, we've flown far more often than we've crashed.

Trust Ritual for Lovers

This small ritual was sent to me by Rachel, Giovanni, and JT, a poly-amorous triad in Florida. They stressed that it evolved spontaneously one day and that they repeat it rather spontaneously every now and then. One of them, for whatever reason, will say the first line, and it will signal the others to follow. "It's become our personal ceremony, used to bind us together when times get tough," says Rachel. "We're including it because it might help other polyamorous families if they try it."

The rules are these: One person speaks each line—anyone, it doesn't have to be the same individual each time—and it is echoed back to them by each other person. If one lover does not feel, for some reason, that he or she can say the lines with a whole heart, he or she gets up and leaves the room. This is a signal that they have issues that need to be discussed; the other members should drop what they are doing and follow along in order to have a discussion. This ritual should not be attempted somewhere people can't leave, such as a moving car on a road trip.

First, one person says, "I trust you." Everyone echoes.

Second, someone says, "I trust that there is no malice hidden between us and that you would tell me now if it were so."

Third, someone says, "I trust you to remember how much I love you." Everyone echoes.

Fourth, someone says, "I trust you to remember my needs and desires." Everyone echoes.

Fifth, someone says, "I trust that when you hurt me, it's an acci-dent." Everyone echoes.

Sixth, someone says, "I trust that you want to make it up to me." Everyone echoes.

Seventh, someone says, "I trust that no matter what happens, we are family." Everyone echoes, and everyone should touch each other in some way, if only clasping hands together.

PART III

Water

The Chain of Emotions

The element of water is associated with the free flow of emotions, whether comfortable or uncomfortable. Water can be overflowing joy or a torrent of tears; the reviving drink of love or the drowning depths of despair. It should go without saying that in the practice of love, water is the crucial element, the one without which no love relationship will get very far. It should also go without saying that the emotions cannot be brushed off or belittled when it comes to polyamory.

The water stage is the third stage of relationship, the one where the fire has burned down and the lovers are beginning to merge and flow together. It is the stage of opening up the deeper places in the heart, and that's often painful. In the air stage, we believe in the instant intimacy we've created by telling each other our stories, but we still don't fully trust them, and we secretly feel that we can still hide our flaws from this new person. In the fire stage, this falsehood is revealed and burned away, and what's behind it at the end of all those ashes is the endless throbbing sea of our wounds and pains and joys. This is the point when we realize that the instant intimacy of the air stage was a shallow thing and that there is still much more to this person than we ever understood. Sometimes we welcome that knowledge, and sometimes, if it shows us someone quite different than we were led to believe, we flee from it.

If we don't run away, we are forced to learn to trust them and to convince them to trust us. If a relationship survives the fire stage, it still has a good chance of failure at the water stage, because trust is never an easy thing. It is, however, the ultimate basis of polyamory. Without trust, the practice is doomed to failure. This means a lot of emotional processing, whether you like it or not. In fact, it's not often a likeable thing, but it is always a necessary thing. If anyone's feelings are being disregarded, it can all blow up.

In most of Western society, we're taught that feelings are irrational things that should be put aside, or better yet excised, if they get in the way of doing anything. It's not acceptable to make decisions based on your feelings. People do it all the time, of course, but they find various words to justify it and pretend that their decisions were made through logic. On the other hand, in some modern alternative subcultures, feelings are put far above thinking, ideals, or commitments, as a sort of backlash, and it is acceptable to blow projects and people off if keeping your word might entail a great deal of discomfort. The balance point between emotions, thoughts, and commitments is a difficult place to find, and one has to start with actually being honest about what one is feeling before one can make any decision to honor or override it.

Oberon Zell-Ravenheart explains: "We have always accepted Robert Heinlein's definition of 'love' as 'that condition wherein another person's happiness is essential to your own.' We genuinely care first and foremost about the happiness of our partners, however many there may be. Liza came up with the concept of a 'Conspiracy of Heart's Desire.' Thus, our entire family is continually engaged in a conspiracy to create the fulfillment of Heart's Desire for each other. And we truly believe that 'With love, all things are possible.'"

They find that their best tool is "a commitment to openness and honesty in our relationships. This is absolutely essential to polyamory. It means that if our feelings are being hurt, we tell each other. And if we know that our lovers' feelings are hurting, we drop everything to take care of them and do whatever is necessary. Often, feelings are hurt and jealousy activated when we feel that we are not getting the attention we need. If that happens, then we make a special effort to give each other that attention. We take each other out to dinner and movies, have special romantic dates and evenings, bring each other flowers and little gifts, and in general try to shower each other with love and affection. This is made easier by having more people involved. As we say, sometimes it's necessary to call in reinforcements!"

One thing that people in polyamorous relationships run into is the problem of feeling-type people and thinking-type people processing emotions differently. This is something that a monogamous couple can also run into—there can be one feeling-type and one thinking-type there as well—but there's also a good chance that there are two of the same type. The more people you add, the more likely it is that you'll end up with a mix of people who process their emotions differently and will have to adapt to each others' styles in order to negotiate properly.

When I refer to "thinking-type" or "feeling-type" people, I don't mean to suggest that thinkers don't have emotions or that feelers don't have brains. On the contrary; some of the feeling-type people I've met have brilliant minds, and some of the thinking-type people I've met are remarkably insightful and articulate about their own feelings or those of others. These terms simply refer to someone's natural default. In a crisis, are they more likely to fall back on an emotional response or an intellectualized one? Which is more important to them: their ideas or their emotional state? Most people fall into one camp or the other, although a few may live on the borderline. An evolved member of either camp has learned to balance the two, although they will always keep their natural tendency.

In a small group situation, such as a polyamorous relationship, one person or one type may dominate the process and may make people of the other type feel that there is something wrong with them because they aren't comfortable doing it that way. Sometimes they may even verbally tell the non-dominant type that there is something wrong with their way of processing feelings, which simply makes them close down and helps no one. It's often a useful thing to identify the thinking types and the feeling types in your poly family and figure out if one type is trying to run things their way, without compromising or devaluing the other way of doing it.

Sometimes the culprit is a thinking type using logic as a battering ram, telling the feeling type(s) that their feelings are ludicrous and irrational and should be dismissed or excised. This works exceptionally well if the dominator is either a) extremely articulate and an excellent debater; b) has learned enough jargon to be able to sound like they're talking about feelings when actually they're speaking impersonally, or c) male, and able to call on a subconscious social idea that men are intellectual while women are "only" emotional and irrational. (This last one only works if there are no feeling-type men in the poly family to call them on their prevarications.) With this dominator, everything that anyone else says is subject to being used to prove how screwed up they are, intensity is cast as immaturity, and people's words end up getting censored on the basis of how well formed, logical, or graceful their thoughts come out.

On the other hand, the culprit may well be a feeling type. These dominators bury everyone else in the intensity of their overwhelming needs. Everyone else is insensitive, unfeeling, and needs to make allowances for their tender spirits. Everything must be censored on the basis of whether or not it will hurt their feelings, and since their feelings are so easily hurt and so very important, it means that very little gets said honestly. More care is spent phrasing things to avoid the dominator's emotional explosion than in actually getting to the point of a problem. This technique works exceptionally well if the dominator is a) willing to unashamedly make dramatic scenes at the drop of a hat; b) willing to play on people's guilt or their reflexive response to seeing a loved one in pain; or c) female, and able to call on a subconscious cultural idea that women know so much more about feelings that everyone ought to listen to them. (Strangely enough, the presence of a thinking-type female doesn't always counteract this; from what I've seen, I suspect that many thinking-type women are more ready to indict themselves for being flawed if they're not feeling types, and they tend to subside in guilt, hoping that their more emotional sister will show them how to be a "real" woman. Or perhaps they just get shouted down.)

Feeling types have more water and fire in their makeup (and possibly their astrological charts); thinking types are closer to air and earth. All are necessary for life and for a relationship. Each member of the family should declare their type proudly, and then go about the business of learning to appreciate the other type, which is the hard part. For example, Moonflower is a feeling type, and to her, an argument isn't finished until her emotions on the subject are acknowledged. Her two lovers are thinking types, and it doesn't occur to them to do this. When she says, in an angry or hurt tone of voice, "You did X! That was terrible! Don't do it again!" and they say, "Oh, okay, I'm sorry, I won't do it again," they consider the argument over. She stated her case, they considered it, decided that agreeing was the best option for whatever reason, and it's done. She won, right? Back to the video game, right? No such luck.

Moonflower follows them around the house, restating the case again and again, because that wasn't the right response to assuage her feelings. "What's the matter with you? I just agreed to it!" they say. If Moonflower is honest about her needs, she can express to them that they need to acknowledge her complaint and her feelings, as in: "Oh, that clearly made you unhappy. I don't want you to be upset, so I won't do that again. Okay, honey?" This might be accompanied by a small gesture of affection. This makes her feel as if the matter is really settled, and she's really being heard . . . but if she isn't straightforward about her needs in this matter, they won't get met. Of course, it's also up to her thinking-type lovers to refrain from being judgmental about those needs.

Another example might be: Hawk is a thinking type who does a lot of writing, and he has a tendency to say descriptive things when he sees them in the environment. "There's a skunk in the middle of the road." "Your hair has a green cast in this light." "This glass isn't clean." "We need to have another house meeting before Shelley goes away to New York." He doesn't bother to attach any emotional meaning, good or bad, to these comments, because that's not the way he functions. His three lovers are all feeling types, and nothing comes out of their mouths that isn't laden with emotional connotations. Therefore, his descriptive commentaries are scrutinized for random shades of hidden meaning, and when none are found, his lovers supply them from their active imaginations. Usually it ends up with them thinking that he's criticizing them. They have to learn that he really is only stating things from a mental perspective and not an emotional one, and that he's not secretly (or openly) criticizing them . . . even if it *would* be a criticism, or at least laden with subtle connotations, if it came out of their mouths.

Another problem that dogs relationships and can be incredibly annoying to polyamorous dynamics is what a friend of mine calls "birthday present syndrome." Do you remember when you were a child and you were invited to a friend's birthday party? You were taken to the toy store, and you got to pick out a present for them. You chose the best present in the whole store, the toy that seemed wonderful above all, to show how much you appreciated them. In other words, you chose the present that you would have liked to been given. Then you gave it to them with a flourish, and they weren't impressed—maybe because they didn't roller skate, or they didn't like Barbie dolls, or they weren't artistic, or perhaps they'd just hoped for something else. You were terribly hurt, and you didn't understand why they couldn't see that it was the best present in the whole world. And when the time came for them to come to your party, you hoped that they'd give you something just like what you'd given them, and of course they didn't . . . because that was too subtle a hint.

Maybe it didn't happen exactly that way, but often we still reenact that mythical preschool party over and over in relations with other humans, especially when it comes to what makes someone feel loved. If we are not getting from our lover(s) the particular coin that makes our love needs feel paid up, we react by trying to give it to them in the hopes that they'll get the idea and give it to us. It may be even less complex; in our heads, the things that we like are filed as "the appropriate things to show love," and we get upset when we give them and they aren't appreciated, or we get someone else's perfect birthday present instead.

The difficulty is that we like to think that our lovers are our lovers because we have so much in common with them. We would prefer to believe that, among all the other humans in the world, these people are the ones who most understand us, because under all their other differences, they're really a lot like us. Dealing with birthday present syndrome forces us to confront how alien these people that we love really are. If we ask them honestly what makes them feel loved, the answer may chill us with its strangeness. *That* makes them happy? How could that make anyone happy? And how could anyone fail to like what I've been giving? Taking it nonjudgmentally on faith means loving the alien parts of our lovers as much as we love the parts that are like us, and that's not always easy.

In polyamory, a good deal of negotiation is done around finding out what makes each person feel loved and attended to. Sometimes this means that people have to radically alter their behavior and make hard decisions about whether this makes them feel less authentic and whether it's worth all that. Ideally, everyone should be aware of what sorts of things make each other feel loved and wanted, and what sorts of things do the opposite.

Re-Bonding Ritual for After Discussions

This ritual was sent to us by Brenna and Judie from Wisconsin. Sometimes, after particularly difficult or painful discussions, people feel distant and separated from each other. This ritual can help bring lovers back together after such temporary stresses.

Each individual gets a cup and fills it with a different liquid. Brenna says, "Originally we all just used water from our well, but now some of us use milk, or juice, or even wine if we feel that it represents the way that any of us are currently feeling." Over a period of the next hour or so, each person will connect with each other person, and they will offer them their cup and say, "Let me help you." The other person accepts it, drinks, and tells them what would help.

Things to keep in mind: The person being approached should make an honest effort to think of some way in which the person offering can actually do something to make their lives just a little easier. Ideally, it should be something that can be done immediately, does not require a major change ("Stop seeing Joe" or "Make more money" is not appropriate), and won't take more than an hour, because there are others to get to.

The person doing the approaching should refrain from trying to suggest things. If the other person is temporarily wrapped up in their own angst and is having trouble shaking their mind free enough to think of something, it can be very tempting to just accept the offer of a backrub, even if it's not what they want and they have to grimly endure it. There's also that we tend to offer things that are easy for us and don't stretch us, and it may be a good thing to have to live up to a lover's challenge once in a while.

It's also good to try to rotate rather than just swapping off. If Joe offered his cup to Star and then helped him with the dishes, it's better for Star to offer his cup to Jean than to turn around and offer it in turn to Joe. This reinforces that they are part of a poly family, not just a reciprocal couple. However, sometimes it's best just to offer it where your intuition suggests. Go with the flow of feeling on this one, but make sure that you take into account all the different flows and not just your own and that of whoever's eyes you're currently looking into.

Moon
Family and Children

"For the past year, I have been dealing with the Department of Social Services, the Department of Mental Health, the Child Assessment Program and a few others of the alphabet soup of government agencies in order to prove that my daughter did not belong in foster care. I never lied to them about anything. I told them up front about the fact that I was polyamorous and that I had multiple lovers.

"During one of the many meetings that I had with these people, I tried my best to explain yet again what polyamorous really means. No, I did not have a revolving door on my bedroom, nor did I have hot and cold running lovers in multiples each evening, nor did I do intimate things in the living room in front of my eight-year-old daughter. I told them how one of my partners had been part of my life—and my daughter's life—for seven years at that point, even though it had been more than two years since we had actually had sexual relations. Her daughter and mine consider themselves sisters, and when my girlfriend lost her home, her daughter came to live with us for about two years. I explained that my other lover and I were physically intimate on a less than monthly basis, even though we lived together and shared a bedroom. Unfortunately, their idea of nonmonogamy pretty much equated to child abuse, due to 'inappropriate behavior in front of a minor.'

"I explained to them repeatedly how polyamory is, in my opinion, not only better for the adults involved, but also healthier and safer for the children. In our household there were three children and four adults. When one of the adults was busy, there were always a few more to seek help from, someone to watch the other children while a crying child had their skinned knee bandaged, someone who wasn't too busy for an extra snuggle. The adults had each other to rely on when the stress of three happy screaming children playing became a bit too much and they needed a break.

"The people I was speaking to looked at me as if I had three heads. I waxed poetic about the joys of like-minded people raising children in concert, the love from more than just a single- or double-parent household that was there for these kids. I likened our household to the old days when a household consisted of more family members than just mom, dad, and offspring—in some families there were grandparents, aunts, or cousins. I could see blank looks on their faces.

"Finally, the meeting ended, and I got up to use the bathroom, certain that I had failed to make them understand. On my way to the ladies' room there was a bulletin board like you find in many work-places, filled with funny signs, apartment ads, pictures of new kittens, and the like. One piece caught my eye—a paper with a long description of how geese live. It spoke of how they are always there to help each other, and how when they fly in formation, if the lead goose tires, another goose will pull up and take the lead so that it can go to the end and rest for a while. This sign had been put up to promote the idea that many folks working together is more effective than flying on your own.

"I took it down and went tearing back to the room. 'Read this!' I told them. 'This, right here on your own wall, this explains what polyamorous parenting is really about!'

"I think this may have finally gotten through to them, because even though I told them that I had no intention of giving up my relationships to please them, even though I have taken my lovers to meetings with me, I have managed to prove beyond the shadow of a doubt that I am a good parent to my daughter. This month I will be having the final meeting with the DSS; our case is being closed favorably. Who knows where this could lead? More tolerance for polyamory? Let's hope so."

—RUTH, POLYAMOROUS PAGAN PARENT

In astrology, the moon is the planet of emotions and the inner self. It also rules that most emotional time of life, the parent-child bond, and parenting itself. Polyamorous parenting does seem to be one of the topics that gets everyone emotional, at any rate, when discussing the various merits of the lifestyle. Critics of polyamory worry that children will become confused by having more than two parents around. Defenders retort with lines about it taking a village to raise a child and that they are creating their own carefully chosen village based on bonds of love.

And if you pick the right people, that's exactly what it can work out to be. Although every child is different, most of the kids I've met who have poly parents actually like having all those extra adults around to pay attention to them, if only for a few minutes. My own daughter has been friends with all my secondary partners and has always appreciated the extra attention.

Today, with serial monogamy the most popular relationship form in this country, children frequently have to cope with various stepparents, stepgrandparents, and stepsiblings anyway. It's not that different in the end, except that the parents don't have to break up in order to bring in the stepparent. Mark, a teenager from D.C., relates mournfully that "I went through my parents divorcing, basically because Mom fell in love with a new guy and went to be with him. It was hell. Later, both my parents ended up poly, and I remember yelling at them, 'If that's all it was about, why didn't you just move your new lovers in?' I know that divorce is always more complicated than that, but if they'd just been poly from the beginning, maybe we all could have lived together and I wouldn't have to deal with visitation an hour away."

If the parents are already polyamorous, it can even soften the effect of a divorce, especially when there are extra adults to talk to. Eighteen-year-old Jess of Massachusetts relates, "My mom and my dad got a divorce, but I still had plenty of people around who were good male and female role models, who would pay attention to me when I needed a male or female person to talk to and that parent wasn't available. Because of the polyamory, the group that we considered family was much bigger—lovers and ex-lovers were like extra parents."

Although there are some children who have grown up from birth in polyamorous families, most of the children of our respondents were conceived in prior relationships, and their first view of polyamory was that of "extra" stepparents. The question of who and what their relationship would be was thus hardly any different from that of any stepparent and stepchild who have to work out the delicate dance of their relationship. For my own daughter, the hardest thing for her was bonding to my poly lovers and then having them vanish when we broke up. Of course, this would have been no different if I was a divorced serial monogamist, and she didn't bond to every human being who came through the door, being the suspicious little Scorpio that she is. In fact, when I actually did marry a second time, she had a good deal of adolescent friction with her new stepmother (which we were assured was normal behavior), and she kept openly encouraging me to take on new secondary lovers, perhaps in the hope that I would find one of them more attractive than my wife. She would sometimes flaunt how much she liked them, again simply in order to yank Bella's chain, but as she passed into late adolescence and began dating herself, these behaviors faded away entirely.

She did establish a strong relationship with one of my lovers, a musician who came into my life for three years and with whom I parted on very good terms. She was three when we met and six when we parted. At the same time, we'd made good friends with a woman who, when she heard that my daughter had never had a paganing ritual at birth, offered to be her goddessmother. She was thrilled, and then asked me if my recent ex could be her goddessfather. I asked him, and he was honored. When I remarried, my daughter had at first agreed to be in the wedding party, but at the last minute she changed her mind, feeling shy. Her goddessfather arrived, discovered that she was unexpectedly free of duties, and recruited her to play guitar with him for the reception, giving her a chance to contribute in a less public way.

The moral of the story is that poly stepparents, if chosen as carefully as you'd choose any person who will be dealing with your child, can be very important and useful to any kid's development. Oberon Zell-Ravenheart points out that "I consider it quite an honor when Zack introduces me to his friends as 'my dad.' Being a poly stepparent is sort of like being a beloved uncle (like Uncle Fester of *The Addams Family*); you're not primarily responsible for discipline, but rather the mentorship aspect—introducing them to cool things, providing educational experiences, doing home schooling, etc. Non-biological parents can often be deeply involved in coming-of-age rituals, as well as much of the deep personal counseling (such as feelings around sex) that kids may be reluctant to discuss with their biological parents."

Jess from Massachusetts says, "I know that my lifestyle is unusual, but I feel like having all those wonderful people around me as a kid broadened me and helped me to be a more functional human being. It wasn't just my parents who raised me, it was a whole tribe, and now that I'm an adult, I feel that I was gifted by their presence. These people taught me how to play guitar, how to drive, how to balance my checkbook, how to do beading, how to knit, how to babysit small children, and other skills. They taught me, without directly teaching me, how to respect other people's boundaries and philosophies. No home is perfect, but if I had to do it all over again, I would still have it the same way."

One question that gets asked is what the children call the parents' lovers, which, like the issue of stepparents, is an individual one. Some call them by their first name, some by "aunt so-and-so," some by nicknames. Most feel that it's best that the children choose what they are going to call their parents' partners, especially if they are old enough to talk about it. Ruth says, "My daughter calls my two primary partners Mom as well—Mama Lizzie and Mama Xia. She's also called a few past lovers Mom. She has extra grandparents. She has only one father. These designations are her choices." Similarly, the young daughter of her girlfriend and the young son of her husband's girlfriend referred to her as "Mama Ruth," as opposed to just "Mama," which referred to their own biological mothers.

Of course, there is the issue as to whether the parent's lover should have a relationship with the child at all. When you're a dating parent, poly or not, you have the issue of finding people who appreciate the fact that you're a parent and that this is one of the most important things in your life. In the polyamory contract that I wrote up with my wife, one of the points covers the fact that we would not bring in anyone as a secondary who disliked my daughter. Being mean or rude to her, in or out of my presence, was grounds for immediate expulsion. My various secondary lovers dealt with this in different ways. Some, with whom I was more casual, were friendly but distant. Some who were looking to be more than casual would set out to "woo" her, which was not an easy goal, considering her generally suspicious nature. (Either way, she always got lots more gifts at Yule.) My current secondary partner gets along very well with her, as they share musical interests and occasionally swap clothing.

I laid down a few ground rules for controlling her interactions with my secondary lovers and with any primary lover I had after divorcing my ex. First, I stressed that any discipline and any decisions about her life were to be made only by her biological parents. If my other lovers had an issue with her behavior, they were to come to me and I would handle it. This kept the incidence of "You're not my parent and you can't tell me what to do!" to a minimum. Second, I never left them to babysit her until we had been dating for several months and it was clear that they were both enthusiastic about the idea. It's better to shell out for someone less involved to come over than to stress the relationship too much. Third, I took her seriously if she began to have issues with them. Mediating between child and lover is much like mediating between lover and lover—it's necessary, and it's your job if you're the parent—except that the child's needs are more important. Fourth, I made sure that no lover that moved in displaced her physically. She had her own room and her own things, and I refused to let their belongings impinge on her space.

PolyPagan of the Waterkin from New Zealand also stresses that having enough space for everyone is important. "We have a large house with plenty of room for all three children and all three adults to be able to be together or have their separate space. That way partners can bonk, sleep, and spend time with one another just as we feel like it, entirely spontaneously. Sometimes we bonk as a triad; mostly two of us sleep together. But the space is important." They have had no issues with their children relating to society as of yet: "The kids' natural parents are two of us, but they relate to us as being their three parents. They know it's unusual, but have no problems with it at all except in trying to explain our family to their friends, so they usually just skirt around that and go play their games."

Another issue that many people worry about when mixing polyamory and children is the idea that they might not know who their biological parents are. From what we've seen, in every case the children are quite well aware who spawned them. In cases where the secondary partner has been around since they were small (or since before they were born) and co-parents them, they are still aware of where the genes came from. It just doesn't matter as much to them.

On the other hand, there were a small number of polyamorous Pagans who deliberately obscured the actuality of the child's biological origins. One polyamorous family of three close lovers decided to conceive a baby together; the woman alternated sleeping with both husbands, so that there would be no way to tell the biological father of the child. All three are committed to raising their daughter, and they have a unique system whereby all of them take shifts as the caretaker in charge. They refer to it as doing a shift as the "POD," or parent-on-duty.

Another polyamorous family who preferred to remain anonymous told us that "we've conceived two children so far, and they have two mothers and two fathers. My sister-wife can't get pregnant, so I've taken on the job of having children for both of us—no, all four of us. I don't know whose child is whose, although I have a good idea from looking at them. It doesn't matter, anyway—they both belong to all of us."

Being polyamorous and Pagan means that you are automatically members of two socially unusual subcultures, and that alone can sometimes bother the sort of child who desperately longs to be "just like all the other kids." However, this is the same problem that any parents have who are not mainstream in some way, whether due to polyamory, nonheterosexuality, or being the only Jewish family in the Catholic town, or the only black family in the white neighborhood. Oberon Zell-Ravenheart of California related: "Morning Glory, Diane, and I raised three kids together (one each of a previous marriage) during our ten-year triad marriage. They all got along famously and still regard each other as brothers and sister. Two of them were perfectly happy with being part of a poly family, but one was a little uncomfortable about the whole thing and wanted badly to be part of a 'normal' family, which was not an option. However, this was not about the polyamory issue per se, but more about being poor hippies, which got associated with polyamory in their minds."

It's common knowledge among many other subcultures, including people of color, queerfolk, and other religious minorities, that it's best to teach your child pride in his or her family's difference as early as possible, and never show a lick of shame or doubt about its validity or worth as a lifestyle. Your children will watch you for cues, especially during the early years, and your conviction will become the foundation on which they build their opinions. Teaching them pride in their polyamorous family is as valid as teaching them pride in their minority ethnic heritage or minority faith. The worst thing you can do is hide it from them, telling them that "Uncle Steve" is just a friend of the family. They'll figure it out sooner or later anyway—kids are smarter than you'd think when it comes to that sort of thing—and they'll be unhappy that they were lied to.

"They might tell everyone" is not a good enough excuse either. Even fairly young kids can be told that it isn't appropriate to tell certain things to certain people. Some would say that having any kind of a family secret is a bad thing, but that depends on how it is presented. If the subject to be kept quiet is treated with an air of shame or as if it was bad in some way, children will feel bad about having to keep that secret. If it is stressed that you are protecting the family's perfectly reasonable arrangements from unreasonable and bigoted people who might make trouble, children can feel much better about keeping their mouths shut.

Jess from Massachusetts had one telling point, from the standpoint of a child raised in a poly family: "If I have to give one piece of advice to polyamorous parents, it's this: *Do not lie to your children about your practices.* I cannot stress this point enough. I am horrified when I hear stories about people who refer to their lovers as 'Uncle

Bob' and pretend that nothing is going on between them and the parent. The kids will eventually find out, and then their trust in you will be damaged."

One big worry of the anti-poly line of thought is the idea that if children grow up seeing polyamory as a normal option, they may well decide to be polyamorous themselves. Some polyfolk, especially those whose children grew up in poly households but who are quite monogamous, scoff at the idea. They compare it to children of gay and lesbian parents, most of whom turn out heterosexual. Children make their own decisions as adults, they say, and point to various grandparents and friends as monogamous role models. However, our little demographic study saw a different picture. Unlike inborn sexual preference, polyamory is a cultural behavior that can be learned . . . and just as the anti-polyfolk feared, more than half of the over-14 children raised in poly families are now polyamorous themselves.

Of course, the real question is: why is this a bad thing? If the reason why so many beginning poly relationships fail miserably is—as most polyfolk claim—that people aren't prepared to handle it and are not taught the relationship tools necessary to cope, then growing up in a poly family ought to give one a boost in that area. Do children who watch their parent group process and negotiate learn those skills better than those who only have two parents, possibly caught up in bad social patterns of how marriages ought to go, as role models?

The Ravenhearts believe that it's true: "All our kids have gone on to form excellent relationships, and I do believe that their experiences around our poly dynamics have helped them in this. They have learned how to relate honestly, communicate, live together, make compromises, mediate disputes, and have fun. Many of the young people who have grown up in our larger community have, in fact, adopted polyamory as their chosen lifestyle, which they seem to be handling very well. And some have chosen monogamy and are doing well there. The whole point all along is to have that choice."

The children I interviewed who grew up in polyamorous families all seemed very clear on both the fact that sex was involved between the polyamorous adults in the house and that, conversely, polyamory was rarely just about sex. Sean, age eighteen, told us: "My mom believes that polyamory should have an emphasis on the 'amory.' To her, it means that there will always be someone there for you when you fall, no matter what happens."

Jess in Massachusetts claims that "I am happily and unrepentantly polyamorous. I'm second-generation poly. Because I grew up watching it, I knew how it was supposed to be done. When I needed advice, I could go to my mom and say, 'What should I do?' and get a helpful answer that worked. I managed to avoid most of the pitfalls that beginning poly people get themselves sucked into. If I'd grown up in a monogamous family, I'd probably still be polyamorous, but I would have stumbled over every pitfall in the book. I did try my hand at monogamy, but it didn't work. I'm still friends with that lover now, but I feel bad for not living up to her expectations and being unable to make the monogamy work. It just wasn't who I was. Being a person growing up around polyamory, I was quickly able to realize that I was not monogamous before we became too committed; it would have hurt her deeply to realize that our relationship was a lie."

She also related that in her teenage relationships, she was generally the one with more stringent expectations and boundaries. "Because I grew up polyamorous, safe sex has been hammered into my mind since before I became sexually active. I've always been the one to explain—and to demand—safe sex, communication, and painful honesty from my lovers. From watching the people around me, I've learned that whatever you say, it hurts more when you lie."

Just because you've been the long-time lover of a parent, and a co-parent to their child, doesn't mean that you will have any rights to that child should their legal parent die, unless legal documents are drawn up to that effect. Some of the polyamorous parents, especially those who were in long-term live-in family situations, pointed out that one of the benefits of their lifestyle was knowing that no matter what happened to them, there would still be a family to take care of their children. For some, these bonds remained even after the sexual ones faded. Ruth in Massachusetts tells of an ex-girlfriend with whom she is still friends, and whose daughter she was very close to: "There is paperwork drawn up in case she dies; her daughter will come to live with me should that happen. She trusts me more than she trusts her relatives, who are abusive."

Other polyamorous parents have drawn up legal paperwork to make sure that in the event of their deaths, the poly spouses will have access to visitation rights. Unfortunately, most of them admit that they know those papers could be overturned if custody went to a particularly bigoted relative. "I do worry about what would happen if one or two of us die," admitted an anonymous poly woman from a family of four. "My mother has said already that we're all living in sin and that if it weren't for the fact that my husband and I were legally married—and we have a good income from four paychecks— she'd go to court and try to have our kids taken away."

When it comes to legal battles, being both Pagan and poly- amorous does put one doubly at risk. As Ruth's story at the begin- ning of the chapter shows, social service agencies do not look kindly on people with unusual relationship arrangements. They don't tend to look kindly on Pagans either; there have been many issues in even the relatively liberal state of Massachusetts with social workers who believe that Pagan equals satanic equals child sex abuse. I've had monogamous friends whose children were snatched due to their Pagan practices; I can only imagine what would have happened if there were other lovers involved.

However, the ignorance and unfairness of society and govern- ment is not a good reason for refraining from having the relationships that you desire. That's rather like saying that no one with children should be actively gay, because in some states they can take the kids away. Yes, they can, but that can only be solved by brave people who are willing to take the bull by the horns before they get gored. It would be a good thing if both Pagans and polyamorous people approached the local DSS, or whatever it's called in your state, and offered to do educational workshops for the workers. Those of you without children to snatch can go first and pave the way for those with kids. In fact, if there's one thing that you'd like to do in order to improve lives of polyfolk in this country, that's it.

Pre-Handfasting Polyamorous Adoption Ceremony

This ritual was sent to us by Judie in Wisconsin; it was created by her sister-wife Anatolia when she joined a female couple as their third and brought her young daughter with her. All three adults felt that since they were committing to each other as a family, it was important to commit to helping Anatolia raise her daughter, the most important person in her life. Stephanie had lost her father and both grandmothers to illness and death and was feeling as if she had little family left. It meant a great deal to her to be joining a family that would promise to stick around.

Judie says, "The ritual was done in the kitchen, which was the center of our home. First we smudged her with burning sweetgrass for fire and air, and then put henna on her hands in a design for earth and water. We all blessed her, and we took a big soda glass and put it on the kitchen table. Each of us added something to the glass, creating a float for her to drink at the end." Her mother and her mother's partners said the following words:

Mother: Stephanie, when I was looking for people to spend my life with, I looked for three main things in them. First, that they would love me and treat me right. Second, that I would love them and feel kinship with them. Third, that they would love you and see you as a special person, as I do. The first two weren't enough; I wouldn't settle for less than all three. And I think I've done a pretty good job here—two for the price of one!

I hope you know that I don't love you any less just because I now have more people to love. I also hope that being part of this family will help you through any more hard times in your life. I'm adding vanilla ice cream to this glass for you. It's made of milk, and I gave you your first milk from my breast when you were a baby and poured your first cup of milk when you were a toddler. In the name of the Great Mother, may you be nourished. I love you, and I'm proud of you.

Partner #1: Stephanie, you didn't grow inside my womb, but your presence here has grown inside my heart. I'm not ever going to have any children of my own and that troubled me. When I decorated this house, I would paint flowers and cats on the wall and think, "Wow, some kid would love this." And then I'd remember that I could not have children, and I'd be sad. And then when you moved in, you asked for the room with the flowers and cats. It made my heart lighter to know that those flowers and cats were doing what they were supposed to do. You were like the Maiden Goddess, bringing a breath of spring into this house.

By bringing you into our family, we are stretching our family to hold the next generation. I hope that someday, when you're grown, you'll bring more children into this family, either by having them yourself or by bringing in someone else who has children that need a loving family. But that will be your decision and that of the hand of Fate. I am giving you this silver chain, because it symbolizes the links between us and between our kin and friends and future members of this family. I want you to know that now that you're part of us, you will also have a say in who we choose to bring into this house to live.

I'm adding strawberries to this glass to symbolize sweetness and summertime. May it always be summer between us, even when it's winter outside. In the name of the Maiden Goddess who watches over you, may you be nourished.

Partner #2: Stephanie, when I first met Anatolia, I was worried about the fact that she had a child. I'm a pretty grouchy person sometimes, and I was afraid that just by being myself, I'd hurt your feelings and make your life miserable. I guess I saw you as fragile, because you'd lost your father and you were in a new situation. But I found, to my delight, that you're tougher than that. I also found that having you around makes me less grouchy sometimes, and that's a blessing. The only other things that make me less cranky are my lovers, my garden, my pets, and my music. So you are right up there with Judie, your mom, flowers, kittens and puppies, and Pink Floyd, as far as I am concerned.

I'm honored to know you and to have you be a part of my life. I want you to be in my family as long as you want it. I'm giving you this stone to wear on your new chain, because you are as strong as stone and as pretty. This stone is amethyst, because I know that one thing we have in common is that purple is our favorite color. It looks delicate, like it might shatter, but if you squeeze it you find that you can't break it, just like you.

I'm adding seltzer to this glass, because it occurs to me that someone ought to add some fizz with all this sweetness around. In the name of the Old One, may you be nourished.

Everyone: Welcome!

The rite ended by everyone cooking a meal together in the kitchen as a family, with the meal consisting of Stephanie's favorite foods.

Venus
Sexual Ethics

In astrology, Venus is the planet of love, beauty, and romance . . . and, of course, the sexual expression that comes with those qualities. While most of the active respondents emphasized again and again that sex was not their main reason for being polyamorous, nearly every one of them was actually having some sort of sexual relations with more than one person. Sex might not be their *raison d'être*, but it was certainly happening. While it's a nice thought that one could treat the negotiation of sexuality with the same comfortable casualness that one treats negotiation of taking out the garbage, in practice it doesn't generally happen that way. Sex is an ambivalent subject that invokes a great deal of passion in people . . . and well it should. The love goddesses will not be treated casually, and too little respect for their power triggers their wrath.

One of the biggest ethical issues in this age of rampant venereal disease is that of safe sex—how to discuss it, how to prove it, and where to draw the lines. Some of the most heated arguments I've heard of between multiple partners have been over whose body fluids get to go into whom and under what circumstances. This is a special problem when people of different ages and from different demographics collide. Folks who went through their sexual awakening more than two decades ago may not be as used to safe sex as the younger generation, who became sexually active already knowing that sex could kill. Even those who are under forty, but who went quickly into monogamous relationships where safe sex wasn't an issue, discover when they start dating again due to divorce or poly- amorous experiments that they have a lot to learn.

All of the polyamorous folk that I talked to had at least some knowledge of safe sex and some regulations around it, but some were cursory and based entirely on trust. Shanna from Arizona says that "safe sex isn't an issue for us. He uses condoms, I use condoms. We know that each of us are being safe, and since our activities with other people are pretty ordinary—we both really only want straight intercourse with heterosexual partners—it's no big deal. I'm one of those people who'd rather not know or meet who Paul is having a one-nighter with anyway, so as long as he tells me he's being safe, I trust him."

Karen in New England has a similar system: "I trust that my hus- band has good sense and that he will use protection, so I don't worry about who he's with or when. The general rule of thumb is that he needs to tell me within a week of when something happens with him and someone new. The reason for the week limit is because we have busy lives and we don't always have the moment we see each other to share things. A week is plenty of time, and it hasn't actually ever gone a week."

Other polyamorous people have very different ideas about safe sex and about disclosure. The Ravenhearts of California report that "safe sex, for us, means our Condom Compact. This means that we each have two circles: the inner one (the 'Compact') in which no condoms are necessary, and the outer one of all other lovers with whom we use condoms. We all take annual STD tests. People can be brought from the outer circle into the Compact after testing by mutual agree- ment of all extant members and by agreeing to that simple rule. Fuckups—which do happen and must be taken into account—are handled with new testing and quarantine periods. We consider oral sex to be 'safe' and don't require condoms for that. We also take into account the actual sexual history of all partners, whether or not they actually have anything transmissible (such as herpes, etc.), and we avoid getting involved with at-risk partners. We discuss these matters with new loves before getting sexually involved with them. Under certain rare circumstances where we have determined that there is simply no risk factor (such as, for instance, with someone who has been celibate for years and tested clean), we have upon occasion allowed a bit of laxity. We have all agreed to these boundaries. There have been issues a few times when people have failed to abide by these rules, and we have had to deal with them."

Joshua in Massachusetts wrote at length about safe sex issues. "My first shot at polyamory was a five-year 'open relationship.' We lived together and had sex with whoever we pleased. We never hid it from each other, but we didn't have any formal requirement to tell each other or ask permission beforehand, and this worked out well for both of us. We had reasonably safe sex with everyone else. That is, we consistently used condoms for intercourse, but had occasional unprotected oral sex. After the beginning stages of the relationship, we didn't use anything with each other. Near the end of the relationship, I began to want tighter body fluid rules. I'd been meeting more folks (especially in the queer community) with a zero-tolerance policy about body fluids. It was hard though. I found I would rather not have oral sex at all than use a barrier, and my partner felt it was just not necessary. We had repeated arguments that seemed to come back to whether the folks my partner had sex with were the 'type' you needed to be so worried about. The unspoken thought was that just because I wanted to have sex with folks that he considered to be disreputable didn't mean we needed to be so paranoid about everyone. I would have preferred a commitment to not swap body fluids with anyone, without these subjective (and often false) judgments on their character, but since I had such a hard time sticking to that rule myself, I didn't feel I could push it on my partner . . . Once we broke up, it was a relief not to be putting anyone else at risk with my questionable behavior. My practices were actually much safer than before, but for once I felt no guilt about not being 100 percent safe. I could make my own decision about what risks I was willing to take with my body and my health. I was reluctant to take up that burden again, but for me sexual intimacy is so bound up with body fluids that I did enter another fluid bond. This time, I demanded a zero-tolerance body fluid barrier and got it."

One Pagan who addressed the issue was a part-time sacred prostitute who also had a full-time lover. This individual gave sexual service in a Pagan temple situation as part of a sacred path dedicated to the love goddesses. She described the difficulties in being both polyamorous and a temple prostitute in this age of STDs. "I'm in a full-time rigid fluid bond with my primary partner, which means that no body fluids can get exchanged when I do my temple work. It is so incredibly difficult for me to have sacred sex while maintaining a safe separation between me and the other person's bodily fluids! But I have no choice. I did safer sex education for a while, and in the training they give you answers to the common objections people have to using barriers, but nothing can address this: you must keep in mind at all times the association of their bodily fluids with death and disease. No. Their bodily fluids are sacred, and to take them into my body is to show ultimate acceptance of them and the physical product of their sexual arousal. To see this exchange not as a messy unpleasantry but as something desirable and beautiful is an affirmation of the sacredness of the body and of the physical realities of sex . . . The way I've ritually dealt with it is this: When doing sacred sex, I have sometimes taken a small pot of honey and fed my client a dab off my finger and had them do the same for me. I explain to them that it is reckless and disrespectful to our bodies to play without barriers in these times, but this sharing of honey is a symbol of the sacred exchange of fluids natural to sex. To share sexual fluids creates a link between you, just as a blood bond does. It is important to me to emphasize that although this exchange has been made symbolic, it is not because the sexual fluids are inherently dirty or disgusting, and I do what I can to downplay that connection to death. But I am of the age where from the time I was sexual, sex could kill. If I broke that fluid bond, every unsafe sex act would feel like Russian roulette. I'd be constantly thinking: Will this one kill me? Am I still safe? Maybe it is already killing me, and I don't even know it. How can we be sexual and not be aware that we walk this line?"

What is actually considered to be safe sex varied widely among my respondents. The Ravenhearts and over half of my respondents felt that oral and nonpenetrative sex was safe, but others disagreed strongly. Judie in Wisconsin scolded, "When I came into our group marriage, my other two partners had this idea that lesbians were safe, we couldn't get STDs, our practices weren't risky, and our dating pool was clean. I set them straight about that, having been given chlamydia once by a supposedly 'clean' lesbian lover. I got them to use dental dams or Saran Wrap for oral sex outside of our marriage. We're now polyfidelitous, so it is no longer an issue." She also complained about attitudes in the Pagan community: "There are those who feel that Pagans ought to be able to protect themselves against disease with magic—damn, I wouldn't want to be risking my life and that of my lovers while depending on some spell that might or might not work! And then there are the ones who claim that you can't get diseases while in sacred space, which can mean as little as lighting some incense and chanting before you hit the sack. What makes them think that the Goddess loves viruses less than she loves humans? They are all her children, whether we like it or not, and she doesn't play favorites, especially in this age when there are too darn many of us on her green earth. I see the increase in STDs as Gaea's attempts at population control."

Sometimes their ideas of what was safe changed over time, such as one respondent who mourned, "When it was just my wife and myself, we had decided that certain things were an acceptable risk—oral sex, for example, or using fingers and hands. We used condoms, but that was all, unless the other person asked for safer sex, in which case we'd oblige them. Then I got a secondary relationship that became very emotionally serious, and he moved in with us. We agreed to let him into our fluid bond and then discovered that he didn't want that . . . unless we tightened it up. He'd been closer to the queer community, where safe sex is somewhat more draconian, and he didn't feel that our sexual practices were safe enough. Neither of us could see being long-term live-in partners without being able to share in each other's bodily fluids, because we both consider fluid sharing to be a sacred thing, and we wanted to be able to do sex magic together. So it was a choice between him and the looser rules, and of course I chose him. My wife was fine with the rule change; the problem was me. Because of various physical issues, I can't orgasm with a barrier . . . and that's not for lack of attempts with skilled partners! So saying yes to him meant virtual polyfidelity, because there's nothing that another partner can do to me that will get me off now. Our love is worth it, but it's hard, very hard."

The issue of "courtesy testing" is a tricky one. Some polyamorous folk swear by them and get regular tests every six months or every year as a courtesy to their lovers, or they get them immediately upon getting a new regular lover and expect the same treatment in return. Others point out that "it doesn't matter if you got tested last week and were clean; you could have had unsafe sex three hours ago for all I know. In this day and age, you can't trust anyone until you know them long enough to know their sexual habits and to be over the silly-in-love stage so that you can see them clearly." This tart comment came from a respondent in Albany, who told us bitterly that "I've been burned too many times by people who claimed to be clean and weren't. I thought I was being smart by never having penetrative intercourse with my outside lovers, but I was wrong. Some diseases can be spread through contact with the groin area, not just the genitals—I contracted both herpes and HPV that way! These days, I feel as though everyone should be dipped in latex, including myself."

There is also the problem that some free or low-cost clinics won't give out written documentation of STD testing. Some get their results back from labs in groups of fifty to a page, and they don't want to violate the privacy of the other forty-nine people. Some clinics don't want the test results to be used as proof of cleanliness at all, because they don't want to get sued by people who contract diseases from lovers who became infected after the test date because they thought that it was safe. Most won't do a workup of all infectious STDs, only the big ones like HIV, hepatitis, or herpes. In order to get a full STD workup with written results, you generally have to go to a private-practice doctor's office and pay for the full range of tests, which can be expensive. Some groups of polyamorous partners have had class-issue problems around those who are able to pay for such tests and those who aren't. "I can't afford to drop three hundred dollars and get a full workup every six months," one impoverished respondent complained. "If I'm dating someone who can afford it, and they want to bring me into a fluid bond, they can darn well pay for it. It stinks, but latex is cheaper than STD workups in my area, especially when you don't have insurance."

From Swinging to Polyamory

When the average person thinks about having sex with multiple partners, what may actually pop into their head may not be the practice of polyamory but rather the demographic referred to as "swingers," or occasionally "wife-swappers." A few of my respondents had started their nonmonogamous careers in the swinger scene, and hardly any had anything good to say about it. That may not be the case for all nonmonogamous Pagans, but my respondents were pretty much universally negative about their experiences with swinging. Colleen in Maryland says, "My husband and I were both swingers before becoming poly. I found that in the swing scene I felt degraded and either like a predator or prey. I felt that the encounters without love and caring and at least some sort of friendship and/or commitment were soul-suckers. We stopped swinging when we found a community of poly people with whom to learn and love."

Brenna from Wisconsin had a more caustic story. "I got into swinging via my last boyfriend. I'd always been nonmonogamous, so it seemed like it would be a fun thing to do, but frankly I felt like a piece of meat on display in those communities. Under the veneer of naughtiness, those are some of the most uptight people you could possibly imagine. I didn't like it that you weren't supposed to become friends or long-term lovers with anyone; it was all supposed to stay anonymous and unemotional so that no one's marriage would be threatened. That and the emphasis on ordinary heterosexual intercourse as the only 'real sex' made it very uncomfortable for me."

However, the tale does have a silver lining: "Ironically, it did lead to something better. I complained about the swing scene to my boyfriend, who heard from a couple of other friends that Pagan gatherings were great places to find casual sex. We also heard that they were laid-back, accepting, and there was much less of a meat-market mentality. I realize, in retrospect, that the Pagans who read this are going to be cringing at the idea that their religious gatherings are being touted as places to get laid, but I want to tell you all that I'm so glad it happened that way! We didn't know anything about this Pagan stuff, but we figured we'd try it anyway, to see if we could find someone for a threesome. By the time I was halfway through the first festival, I was hooked on Paganism, and I never looked back. I also met my first poly friends through that gathering, and I never went back to swinging. Within three years, I'd dumped my boyfriend and was part of the poly family that I live in today."

Another New England polyamorous Pagan spoke extensively about experiences in the swinging lifestyle before coming to polyamory. "I was clear that I was nonmonogamous long before I ever heard of swinging or polyamory, and I practiced negotiated nonmonogamy as a teenager. My then-boyfriend and I were both interested in casual sex as well as love relationships, so threesomes and swinging seemed like the natural thing. Through this I was also involved in the poly scene and found the demographic there to be a poor fit. They were strongly against the anonymous sex we were both looking for, and I found the vegan feminist hippie political slant alienating. Unfortunately, we were also well outside the swinger demographic. They were in their forties, conservative heterosexual 'professionals,' which means businessmen and their wives, while we were kinky bisexuals in our early twenties. We were both hot commodities in the scene and got as much action as we could want. I knew from the start that a sexually adventurous young bisexual woman would be popular, but my partner was surprised how eager many of the housewives were for a rough-looking trucker with a young man's stamina. After screwing dozens of their husbands, pasty accountants and polished executives with unreliable cocks and little enthusiasm for anything but the old in-out, I could understand their fascination.

"I found the rigidity of the sex roles and the commodification of women to be rather silly, but sillier was the conception of kinky sex. Simply having sex with strangers was terribly naughty to most couples, and the ones who would do it in public at the clubs were 'real players.' Kinky sex consisted of cheap lingerie, role play, and blow jobs, and a 'dominant' or 'aggressive' woman was one who asked for oral sex and liked being on top. Light bondage, sex toys, spanking, or anal sex would get you a reputation as a serious pervert, scaring off many partners but intriguing others. That sort of thing was done very secretively. 'Discretion' was big in all facets of the scene, but even more so with the kinkier sex, meaning that it wasn't even discussed. Bisexuality in men was entirely forbidden, and the 'bisexuality' in women seemed limited to two women getting it on for the amusement of their husbands.

"Outside of the club scene, I did find swingers who were interested in forming long-term relationships as pairs of couples or triads, even to the point of all living together. These often bordered on the New Age swingers, who were much closer to the polyamorous ethic of focusing on love rather than sex. Of course, this love was expressed primarily through group massage, steam baths, and 'Tantric' sex, which in their opinions seemed to consist of hour-long hand jobs done to New Age music. There was a great deal of nudity and recognition of the body and sexuality as sacred, but the range of acceptable activities was even narrower than in the rest of the swing community. The main exception was that men were encouraged to exchange intimate, nonsexual touch with each other, and 'prostate massage' or other forms of anal penetration were acceptable to 'stimulate the root chakra.' The sex roles were just as rigid, but they were egalitarian and openly discussed."

Safe sex practices in the swinging community were, according to my respondents, often loose and iffy. One former member of this scene wrote bitterly that "there's a social group in my area that is mostly swingers, although they will use the polyamory label to seem more touchy-feely. Herpes has spread so quickly through this group that over half of them now have it. They don't disclose it, either, because they consider it a 'nuisance disease,' something that can be easily controlled with medication, so it doesn't matter if their partners catch it. Herpes may seem benign to someone with a normal immune system, but if yours is damaged, from AIDS or leukemia or some other problem, it can spread throughout your body and be a terrible torment. But of course they'd rather not think about that."

The Group Sex Controversy

Polyamorous sex is not just about negotiation and latex. Although most of my respondents put more emphasis on love bonds than on sex, the fact remains that they were actually being physically intimate with more than one person. Most were reluctant to discuss their sexual habits—and to be fair, that's none of my or anyone else's business—but a few brave souls did talk about it. "I know that I'm supposed to emphasize the love aspects of polyamory, or everyone will think that we're just sluts," says Brenna of Wisconsin, "but since I've already done plenty of that in the rest of my questionnaire, I can talk about sex now and not feel guilty. The sex is great. I love group sex. There's something in it that brings me back to a primitive, tribal state—it's like communal food sharing in that way to me. Just as it's sacred to me that we all made the food together with our own hands and might feed it to each other with our own fingers, it's sacred to me that we all sleep in the same bed—which is three beds pushed together—and that we are four bodies in the dark together, four bodies that love each other."

She admits that sex isn't always a group pile: "The most likely group sex scenario for us is that two of us start to get it on. We'll check first to make sure that no one else in the bed needs to get up early and would be disturbed by our lovemaking; if that's the case, we'll hie ourselves off to a spare room with an empty bed. (We have two, plus the foldout couch.) Either the sexual energy raised by those two will entice one or both of the others to join, or more likely they'll just stroke us absently and fall asleep to our noises. If it's going to be really dramatic, cathartic sex, we definitely take it elsewhere—no one can sleep through that. We tried doing the method described by Starhawk in *The Fifth Sacred Thing*—putting one person in the center, everyone makes love to them, and then we switch off—but it takes too long, and the last one to get done is usually burnt out and unhappy. Instead, we've just learned to multitask during sex—to concentrate back and forth on simultaneously giving and receiving. It sounds complicated, but to us it's natural now."

Not all polyfolk have group sex; the majority interacted sexually with their lovers at separate times and places. A few had made limited efforts in that area; Rachel from Florida admits, "Yeah, I'd love it if Gio and JT were comfortable being in bed with me at the same time, but they rarely are. Once or twice a year they'll both jump me, usually for my birthday or if I'm having a really bad time for some other reason. It's incredibly exciting. I do sex magic with both of them, and I'd love it if I could do it with both at once—I can just imagine the energy that it would raise! But they each prefer sex to be time shared between both of us."

Sex magic, for the poly Pagans who practiced it, also seemed to be a two-at-a-time thing with, again, a few exceptions. One poly Pagan family talked about "doing Tantric breathing together, just the three of us, while touching body to body. It's amazing what synchronized breathing can do to raise sexual energy. We were three-quarters of the way to orgasm before the clothes even came off and the touching started. I suspect that if we had even more people, it would be more intense still."

Another trio, who also wished to remain anonymous, told me that one of their favorite sex magic tricks was for two people to make love while the third harnessed the energy and directed it. The best position for this, they had found, was for the two who were having the sexual activity to be in close physical contact with the third person—having their heads in the third person's lap, or lying across the third person's body, propped by pillows so that their weight wasn't fully on them. The third person would keep a hand on each of them, pulling out and channeling the energy into a purpose that had been agreed on earlier. All three had learned this technique, so they could all rotate roles as they wished.

One V triad (a triple where two people are lovers with a third person, but not each other) consisting of two men and a woman told me that "we focus our sex magic through her. She's our high priestess as well as our lover, and we both make love to her at once, and she becomes the conduit through which the energy passes. That means that neither of us gets sexually satisfied until afterwards, because part of the energy comes from us maintaining unsatisfied arousal, and if either of us blows off it will end things too soon. So there's usually a second stage to the process, which is the quieter, softer, more loving time afterwards when we get to finish up."

"The most powerful sex magic that I ever had," recounts Rachel of Florida, "was the one time we decided to make love to a friend for one night, for that purpose. She had been recently raped and wanted to do sex magic to drive the negative feelings from her body. JT and I worked on her for five hours—massaging, smudging, touching, holding her while she cried, calling on the gods, singing to her and to them, painting her body and reconsecrating every part of it, and bringing her to orgasm again and again throughout the ritual. Some of it was rough—she felt that she needed to relive the rape, so that she could bring herself to remember it without panicking—and some of it was gentle. It was a powerful healing experience for her and for us as well. For me, it was a fundamental example of what sex magic is all about. But it wasn't something that could have been done with only one helper; it would have been too exhausting. Actually, I think that two or three more would have been helpful. Goddess forbid that I should ever need something like that, but if I do, I'm glad that my years of polyamory have shown me how and where to get it."

Opening Invocation for Polyamorous Sex Magic

We come here in the name of Aphrodite,

Goddess risen from the salty sea,

Goddess of the salty fluids,

Goddess of the mirror's magic,

Goddess of love and beauty,

That we may drown in the sea of love

And float on waves of beauty.

We come here in the name of Ishtar,

Goddess of the temple of the body,

Goddess of the merging of love and battle,

Goddess of the lioness leap,

Goddess of the sacred dance of fascination,

That we may rise with the flames of passion

And dance in the body's flame.

We come here in the name of Freyja,

Goddess of the golden wheat,

Goddess of the jeweled breast,

Goddess of the smoky mysteries,

Goddess of the armored flight,

That we may know our own value to each other

And comprehend the mystery of love and power.

We come here in the name of Oshun,

Goddess of the honey brandy,

Goddess of the golden coins,

Goddess of the peacock feather,

Goddess of the circling vulture,

That we may recycle our darknesses together

And continually rebirth our love.

We come here in the name of Babalon,

Goddess of the dark secrets,

Goddess of the outcast lovers,

Goddess of the whip and the rod,

Goddess of deep compassion,

That there might be nothing held back between us,

No lies and hidden terrors,

No shields and no walls,

And yet we might come together in acceptance

Of each others' depths and shadows.

We come here in the name of Love,

Ready to be harnessed to Love with golden chains,

Ready to harness Love to our desires,

Ready to walk Love's road,

Ready to be ridden by Love's need.

Love not under will

But partnered with will,

We walk together into the fire.

PART IV

Earth

Building a Home Together

The element of earth, in Neopagan symbolism, relates to stability and all things practical—paying rent, eating food, finding shelter, getting your taxes in, taking care of your body. Although many people may only see polyamory as a matter of negotiation around emotions, those who find themselves in long-term polyamorous relationships discover that a great deal of negotiation also needs to happen around the practicalities of life. This is especially true when it comes to living with more than two partners under the same roof.

"It's all the drama of living in a group house with lots of house-mates, on top of all the usual poly drama," says Rachel of Florida. "Sharing toothbrushes, dividing up household chores, deciding who pays for what home improvement. Who's going to spend what on food—especially when you're all on different diets! Gio and I were vegan when JT moved in, and she's a carnivore who would never agree to stop cooking burgers in our kitchen. We've compromised in that she uses her own pots and pans, but I never thought that I'd have to center a poly negotiation around greasy dishes!"

Not everyone wants to live with all, or even most, of their lovers. Tim from New Jersey writes about his ambivalences in living with his polyamorous lovers: "Just because you love someone doesn't mean that you live well together. Anyone who's tried to be room-mates with a good friend, and found that in six months they weren't good friends anymore, knows all about this. One of the things that I like about being polyamorous is that I don't have to live with all my lovers or even my primary partner. Currently, I live with my secondary, who is legally my wife and used to be my primary except that we both got closer to our other lovers than we were to each other, and her primary lover. We all get along fine as housemates—no trouble dividing up chores, and we all make a good deal of money, so that's not an issue. My wife and I own the house, but they're my family. But my primary lover is a hermit who likes to live alone in the house that she inherited from her parents. So I spend three to four nights a week there—she needs the rest of the time alone to do her art—and the other half of the week at home. Frankly, she's a slob who would drive the three of us crazy, and it's best that she has her own place where she can drop food on the floor and change the cat box only when it gets so bad that I won't come over. This way I get the best of everything—a primary relationship where we don't have to be miserably married and expected to live together, and a nice house-and-family situation with my wife and her boyfriend, who also has no wish to marry."

Oberon Zell-Ravenheart of California admits, "The pros of living together are obviously much greater intimacy with each other in our daily lives. For people who can live together, this is wonderful. But some people cannot live well together, or require greater degrees of privacy, or have other lives and relationships. All of us in the family also have outside lovers whom we see only on special dates or when we travel to distant cities, and those have a specialness because they're not part of our daily lives."

Bills and money are generally the center point of discussions for polyfolk who live together. Ruth in Massachusetts says vehemently, "I will never again share living space with someone, partner or not, who refuses to be involved in the bill-paying process. Family meetings are a good plan for that. Letting people get away with not being involved left me being the person blamed for any issue that came up."

Some poly families, like Brenna and Judie's foursome in Wisconsin, combine their incomes into one bank account. "Two of us work under the table and get paid in cash anyway; one of us doesn't work but stays home and cares for the house—she has a degenerative disease and is on disability—and one of us has a small trust fund and runs a home mail-order business, so it's not like there are lots of paychecks to cash. We've all agreed that 75 percent of our incomes will go into the maintenance of our home and family, which includes not just mortgage and utilities but communal food, house repair, and medical bills. Why so much? Because some months people make a lot and some months they don't. We've all agreed to this because we understand that the reasons some people might make more money than others are entirely random and unfair—privilege, disability, age, etc.—and those of us who are blessed owe it to those who aren't to help them out. Yeah, it's pretty socialist, but it works for us—we all know that we'll be taken care of should something happen, and we all share each others' standard of living."

Other families keep their money separate. Rachel in Florida says that "all three of us have separate bank accounts, even though Gio and I are legally married. We couldn't agree to tolerate each other's spending habits, and we couldn't share a joint account without a huge amount of arguing. It's better now that each of us has their own account. With money, we treat each other like roommates— we're each responsible for our part of the bills. I think that living communally with other people whom you're not married to, lovers or not, is good for every married heterosexual couple. It breaks up the weird dynamic that married couples sometimes have around money, especially around who's obligated to support whom or lend money to whom."

Some poly families aim for a middle ground, like the Ravenhearts of California: "Each member of the family has their own bank account. The family business (TheaGenesis, LLC) pays salaries to all who work in it, and some also have other outside incomes. We worked out a budget over a year or so of carefully tracking and categorizing expenses and then divided the average totals for each month among the number of people, adding a bit for a cushion. We opened a family account for 'The Ravenhearts,' with everyone being a signatory. Each month, each person puts in their share. Family and household bills are paid from the family account, and business-related bills are paid out of the business account. This has worked splendidly, and we have had no conflicts over money issues."

Shanna in Arizona wrote to me: "My husband had a live-in secondary girlfriend for about ten months. The relationship broke up not due to jealousy or poly issues, but due to money. She moved across the country to be with him and couldn't find a new job. Her savings ran out quickly, and we discovered that she was the type who let money run through her fingers. That wouldn't have mattered, except that we soon found ourselves supporting her. There were arguments over what we thought were necessary-enough expenses to give her money. She felt that we were being too parental and that my husband ought to let her live with us rent-free because she was his lover—never mind that the two of us have hundreds of dollars in property taxes! I insisted that she contribute financially or leave, which she thought was pretty cold of me. Finally, she found the job of her dreams, but it was in a different state, so she left. There was just no work for her in our area. I sympathize, but we couldn't take a freeloader, even one who was a lover."

On the other hand, some poly families did support nonworking partners. Ruth in Massachusetts "was supported by my husband, his girlfriend, and my girlfriend, while I took care of the children of all three of us women—no paying for daycare, no leaving the kids with strangers, and no one has to leave work when a kid has to be picked up from school."

Judie in Wisconsin related that "one of my wives is on disability, and it was more than three years while she fought the system to get onto it. We took care of her financially all that time, because she's our wife and our love, and how could we do otherwise? We've promised to love and provide for each other as much as we can. If she

130

hadn't gotten disability, we would have all pitched in to create some kind of home business that she could do. She can't do as much of the household chores, either, but are we going to penalize her for that? Her condition is degenerative, and we're well aware that there will come a time in the next twenty years when she may be bedridden, or at least in a wheelchair, and will need special help till the end of our days. Since there are three other wives in this family, of course we will provide for her, whatever we can. That's what a marriage is for."

Her wife Brenna agrees: "One of the reasons to have shared finances in any marriage is so that people can share a lifestyle. We've had lovers who didn't live in and who varied in their monetary class. It's hard to have a non-live-in lover who is very poor, because you want to help them out with money and that creates all kinds of strangeness and pressure. We've had one of those who nearly became a leech and another who proudly wouldn't take a cent, even if it meant that we couldn't pay her way into a gathering where we all wanted to be together, and she couldn't go. Class and money issues are easier to resolve when everyone just lives together and shares one living standard. That makes me uncomfortable to say, though."

One area in which polyamory and money can clash, especially in a couple who are just starting out with polyamory and are still prone to insecurity issues, is the problem of spending money on other lovers. It's especially acute in a household where a primary couple share finances and consider the bank account to be joint money. If one member of the couple wants to spend money taking a new lover out to dinner and a movie, there may be fireworks over a use of the joint money that does nothing for the other partner. One primary couple who have occasional lovers but no serious secondaries had numerous tussles over this one. It was exacerbated by the fact that the wife had frequent liaisons and made significantly less money, whereas the husband was still looking for the right lover and felt annoyed that so much of his resources were being spent on her fun nights. Their decision might seem a bit draconian to some, but it seems to have worked for them. She asks how much she can spend on a particular date, and he gets to choose her budget. This gives him a feeling of control over the monetary aspect of the situation. If she doesn't agree with his budget, she has to spend the equivalent of the extra on something that will benefit both of them as a couple, and it has to come out of her personal savings. If she blows all her personal savings on lovers, she has to accept his budget or work extra hours to afford her romantic habits. This has kept him from feeling used and her from going overboard with flamboyant, expensive getaways.

Another frequent issue for love tribes who live together is household chores and how they are divided. Some poly families find that, at least in the beginning, more structure is needed to keep people from feeling as if the work is not evenly divided. The Ravenhearts of California have this down to a science: "When we all first moved in together, we asked everyone individually to make up a list of chores that they felt needed to be done and how often. Some were daily, some weekly, some monthly, and some annually. Then we took all those lists and correlated them into charts with a calendrical format. There was a weekly chart which listed all chores down the left-hand side and days of the week across the top; and a monthly chart which did the same for the whole year. These were posted on the bulletin board in our 'Communications Center.' Each person was assigned to a color, and appropriate-colored markers were kept in a cup beneath the charts. Everyone agreed to take on certain chores or to rotate them. When someone did a chore, they marked a check in the box. It was easy to track who was doing what and what wasn't getting done. After a year or so of this, we no longer needed the charts, as the chores had become routine."

The Tashlins of Massachusetts report that "we try to have everyone do jobs they dislike as little as possible, and we try to keep things in balance. Our situation is complicated by the fact that Storm is in college, whereas Fire and Winter work full-time. This has led to a real need to not take advantage of Storm's apparent surplus of free time, which is really more of a lack of a set schedule than a lack of things to do. However, as Winter and Fire are the primary breadwinners, there is some expectation of Storm to do more around the house."

One female poly Pagan confessed quietly to me that having her husband's two new lovers—one male and one female—move in had drastically improved the issue of household chores. "He used to have a lot of attitude problems about what was men's work and what was women's work, but once there were all four of us living together, his lovers immediately insisted on an even distribution of chores for everyone, regardless of gender. It took him aback, but where he used to fight me on it, he couldn't fight them both, especially Jay, who could look him in the eye and say, 'If I can fold laundry and make Jell-O, so can you.' Even if you're not ready for polyamory, I highly recommend living in community to any woman whose husband isn't taking on his fair share of the chores. It's easier when you have a whole crowd of people getting on his case, because it's not just his nagging wife anymore."

Since polyamory is not a legal form of marriage, it does mean that any lovers who are not legally married partners have no spousal rights under the law. This concerns many poly families, including Moira Wolf in Arizona: "I have considered some form of legal action to protect Nite, since in our state, should I die, Storm would inherit everything as my surviving legal spouse. I don't want to see Nite thrown out with nothing. I don't believe that Storm would do that, but if something were to happen to me and Storm both, Nite would have no legal recourse or claim on anything other than his personal belongings, and that bothers me."

One bisexual poly man laughed, "When heterosexual people become poly, they are confronted for the first time by the idea that they might have vitally important relationships that nobody is going to honor legally, much less socially. They find out what it's like to have to worry about who will boycott their commitment ceremony, and what happens if somebody is ill and in the hospital and the lover that they need to see can't get in. Queers have been struggling with these issues for decades. Welcome to the club." He stresses, however, that there are alternatives. "With the exception of petty company issues such as insurance, all the legal benefits of a heterosexual marriage can be created with good paperwork. Get legal help and put it together: medical power of attorney, legal power of attorney, and an ironclad will that states who gets what, including children. If you're a threesome and two partners are married, let the third one—the one with the most to lose—be the executor of the will, if it seems appropriate. Make this will public; give copies of it to your relatives, even the hostile ones, so that they can't say that they didn't know. If they call in a rage, refer them to your lawyer. Most importantly, do these things early in the process, while everyone is hale and healthy."

Some poly families organize as cooperatives, businesses, or nonprofits, especially when most or all of the members work together on a specific goal or small company. The Ravenhearts of California are "legally organized in two ways. First, we are an official Family Nest (a congregational unit) of the Church of All Worlds, and thus we are covered under the church's IRS group exemption. We are also all partners in a limited liability corporation called TheaGenesis LLC, which is the family business engaged in producing and marketing sculptures created by Morning Glory, Wynter, and Oberon."

Like the members of any intentional community, a polyamorous household of people has the option of deciding whether or not to put together a household business or simply have everyone hold down outside jobs. As with anyone in a nontraditional relationship, there is always the question of how closeted to be about your living situation, which is made more difficult when all your lovers live in the same house with you and are equally likely to show up with your forgotten lunch, kiss you on the cheek, and call you "Honey." Some poly families have had to go to a great deal of trouble to remain closeted, including making rules as to who may be seen to be whose partner in what workplace, whose photos can be on whose desktop, and so forth. In light of these difficulties, it's not surprising that most of the live-in poly families have tried the option of family businesses, even if only as a part-time project.

Currently, in my own situation, all three of us have outside jobs, full- or part-time. However, the farm that we live on is a joint venture. It's only a small homestead that sells herbs, organic eggs, and barters for goat milk and cheese, but it has been driven home to me why farmers had large families. In a way, we've replaced the breeding-your-hired-help option with the option of acquiring them as lovers. In fact, one of the biggest drawbacks in finding lovers who wanted to live in and be a part of community with us was the farm issue. Living on the edge of nowhere in a small rural town is bad enough; being expected to help slop sheep and milk goats and weed gardens and (especially) shovel manure was more than anyone wanted to get into. My boyfriend started out as a farm intern (he jokes about being promoted from intern to permanent farm slave), so he was already enthusiastic about living our lifestyle with us. It was ironic that we had to screen for that more thoroughly than for all our sexual proclivities.

Tim in New Jersey writes that "my wife was fired twice for being both Pagan and openly polyamorous. The first time, it was because her (female) boss got religion, and suddenly she and the other gay employee became the symbols of Satan, and both got fired. The gay employee decided to take it to court; my wife just gave up and moved on. At this job, the boss found out that she was poly and decided that meant she was a slut and ought to do it with him. The fact that she was Pagan contributed to this, because it meant that she didn't have a 'nice girl's religion.' When she responded badly to his advances, he fired her. It was a hard decision for her, as she's not willing to be in the closet about either her faith or her husbands. Right now she works for a boss who is from China and is fine with polytheism and multiple spouses, and she is doing fine there—ironic that foreigners treat her better than supposedly progressive Americans."

The Tashlins of Massachusetts have had better luck with outside jobs. Two out of three of them work at an oil-change business, and they report that "once we have gotten through the basic workings of our love lives into people's heads, we are usually treated like any gay employee. This applies to Fireheart too, even though she's not actually in any kind of gay relationship." Spouses of employees get free oil changes, and since two of them work there, they managed to convince the owner to allow their third member to get spouse's privileges, even though he wasn't in any kind of legal relationship to the other two.

Of the poly Pagans that I interviewed who had live-in multiple relationships, about half were living in an all-Pagan household community, and half were living with lovers (or lovers' lovers) who were not Pagan. One wrote to me that her family consisted of "two Pagans (who aren't involved with each other), one Thelemite, one Buddhist, one Taoist, and one poor agnostic, who happens to be my husband. We have to put up a lot of altars, and celebrate a lot of holidays, and make a lot of room for each others' magical and spiritual workings. And the discussions of religion and morality over breakfast never leave us bored!"

If you do have more than one (or more than two) Pagans living in the same house, a house altar is often a useful thing to build, especially if they will be celebrating holidays or doing magical workings together. Many Pagans also have their own personal altars, usually in their own space, so what goes on the house altar will vary. Some Pagans like to put one or two things that belong to each person onto the house altar, in order to make it symbolic of each person in the house. Some encourage the non-Pagans in the house to do so as well, if only for the symbolism. Others feel that anything put onto a house altar ought to be a gift to the household, and the items donated should no longer be seen as belonging to the individuals in question.

Some Pagans, especially ones who celebrate holidays together but do their magic workings separately, or who belong to widely varying Pagan traditions, choose to keep the house altar a strictly seasonal thing, changing the decorations with each holiday. This sort of house altar is used as a focus for group seasonal worship, but nothing more. Others choose to fill it with the figures of deities worshiped by various people in the house; this sort is generally used as a focus for both group worship and personal worship, as people can speak to or petition the patron deities of the family.

One Pagan household built an altar in their common room to the lares and penates, who are respectively the Roman spirits of the household and the ancestral spirits of the members of the household. They named and created their own lares and named particular ancestors as their collective penates, some who were related and some who were merely admired as inspirations. This Roman-inspired ritual was based on their house ceremony.

House-Blessing Ritual

First, a place is chosen for the altar. It can be a permanent setting or a temporary place. If it is temporary, however, you should carefully pack away each figure together and eventually find a permanent place where they can live, preferably in a main room of the house. Each member of the family makes one or more figures out of clay, modeling compound, stuffed cloth, heat-formable plastic, a decorated toilet paper tube, or whatever else they feel is appropriate. Lares are generally small, under six inches, so there's no need to make huge creations. Each one is given the name of some virtue; in both the original ritual and our copy, Latin names were used. A household that preferred to name the virtues in English might not go to that amount of trouble. Here are a few of them:

Lucina (light)

Pax (peace)

Opus (hard work)

Amor (romantic love)

Salubris (health)

Sapiens (wisdom)

Vita (life)

Veritas (truth)

Terra (earth)

Ignis (fire)

Aqua (water)

Caelum (air)

Spiritus (spirit)

Sol (sun)

Luna (moon)

Penates, or ancestral spirits, should be represented by small pieces of paper on which is written something that they were famous for having written, or having said, or would have been likely to say. It can be actual blood ancestors of the people in the house or simply people that they admired who they would like to have as guardian spirits, in the same spirit that Z Budapest's first coven was named after Susan B. Anthony.

Everyone comes before the altar bearing their lares. They should also bear noisemakers, even if only pots and pans to bang on. To open the ritual, have someone say:

May this household be clear of cruel words

And tongues that wag behind backs

And may all its silences be peaceful.

We, its living breath, call out for this!

May this household be clear of wrath,

And smoldering rage, and jealousy,

And the irritations that fall like sparks

To set the dry tinder of boredom alight.

We, its all-seeing eyes, sing out for this!

May this household be clear of sorrows,

And sullen resentments, and floating envy,

And the suspicions that swim in our inner swamps.

We, its heart's blood, cry out for this!

May this household be clear of uncertainty,

And the muddled fall of chaos, and laziness,

And may its tasks divide up equally and fairly.

We, its many bodies, stand as one!

Each person stands forth and places their lares on the altar, one by one, and states their name and perhaps why they felt that this spirit was needed in the household. Everyone repeats the name of each one of the lares, loudly and in unison. Then each person lays down their penates and explains them. A single candle is lit, and everyone says, "So mote it be."

Then a march is taken throughout the whole house, banging and blowing noisemakers. One person has a broom with which they sweep the air to symbolically remove bad spirits. Start at the lowest point and move through to the highest window, making sure to open every closet and sweep it out as well. Beds should be given extra care, as this is often where nightmares start. At the top of the house, open the highest window and sweep everything out. Then go downstairs and have a party.

Saturn

Boundaries and Contracts

In astrology, Saturn is the planet of both obstacles and boundaries, limits and discipline, tradition and repression. Saturn is the force that says, "Eat your vegetables. Pay your bills. Do the correct thing even when it's uncomfortable." Although most people shun Saturn's force and complain about it mightily, a relationship without that influence doesn't tend to go anywhere, because Saturn is the planet of commitment.

I am coming to this chapter revealing a bias of my own: I think that boundaries in relationships are good things, especially if they are stated, negotiated, honest boundaries. It seems that next to poor communication, the second most frequent reason that poly lovers break up is poor boundaries. You can't build a good commitment without them, and even an uncommitted relationship may break up sooner if they aren't clear and open and agreed upon by everyone involved.

The first boundary that most people think of in relationships is that of legal marriage. Since it is not, at the time of this writing, legal to marry more than one person at a time, that means that only one relationship per individual will be allowed legal standing. That doesn't mean that we as Pagans can't make space for multiple-person marriages and take them just as seriously as we do that of couples. In fact, a Pagan clergyperson may be the only hope of a polyamorous bunch who want help with their wedding ceremony and who want a clergyperson that will take them seriously and perform their wedding without a single raised eyebrow.

The most common polyamorous situation, as we've already mentioned, is that of one legally married couple who have one or more other lovers. This is partly because so many people come to polyamory after they're already married, but it can also happen due to a conscious decision by two (presumably heterosexual) members of a poly family who are determined to have at least one lover who can advocate for another one should they be unable to do so themselves. Shanna of Arizona writes, "Originally, I had two men that I both considered my husbands. I felt like I had to marry one of them, because I wanted at least one husband who would be recognized by hospitals, police, and so forth. It took several months of hard thinking to decide which one it was going to be, but all three of us finally settled on Paul, for various reasons. It was a good choice, as I broke up with my other husband a year later. But now Paul is with a woman whom he considers his second wife, and she's got a lot of health problems. It may eventually become necessary for him to advocate for her health, so we've actually considered getting divorced and having him marry her in order to make sure she gets what she needs, although nothing would change between him and me."

Others are ambivalent about poly marriage. PolyPagan of the Waterkin from New Zealand comments: "On the one hand, we'd like to marry our third, but are not allowed to by law; on the other hand, we don't like the involvement of the state in our personal relationship at all."

The Neopagan custom of trial handfastings—such as the classic "year and a day" handfasting or the vaguer "so long as love shall last" version—can work well for polyamorous additions. YuleCat of Massachusetts chuckles: "A and I did a traditional year-and-a-day Pagan handfasting before getting legally married. I jokingly referred to it as the '366-day no-money-back guarantee.' But the concept of a year-and-a-day commitment that would be up for review at the conclusion very much appealed to both of us. Having failed at long-term relationships in the past, this let us ease our way into one with each other and gave us a way out if things didn't work."

Legal marriage, at least between heterosexuals, seems to be the classic way that primary partners commit to that primary status with each other. YuleCat again: "One of the many reasons that A and I got married was to firmly establish ourselves as each others' primary, in our own eyes as well as those of any additional partners, present or future. I'd had a couple of secondary partners attempt—unsuccessfully—to steal me away from A. The fact that I'm now married seems to have deterred any further attempts. Either that or I don't go after those kinds of women anymore."

He has also decided on a unique way of symbolizing his secondary lover: "B and I wear identical rings on our right hands, kind of like the wedding rings that each of us have on the left hand. In addition to the significance of these rings to ourselves and each other, they also provide an easier way to explain the significance of our relationship. The symbol itself says a lot."

Even without marriage or long-term handfastings, boundaries are necessary to make sure that everyone knows what they can expect from their lover(s). The Ravenhearts of California say: "As to our boundaries, we have a notion of prioritizing our primary relationships if a conflict should arise. Primary partners have an ultimate veto over secondary relationships that they may feel are destructive or inappropriate to their relationship. We make a real effort to bring home prospective new partners and introduce them to the whole family, usually inviting them to a special dinner and evening. We discuss prospective new relationships with our partners and get feedback and approval. We have our boundaries around safe-sex issues and have worked out parameters we are all comfortable with. We help mediate with each other when that's needed, and we commiserate with each other over relationships that aren't working out."

As we mentioned in Part I, the terms "primary" and "secondary," and sometimes even "tertiary," are both widely used and widely debated. Some polyfolk swear by them; Joshua in Massachusetts says, "I like the terms because they help me know where I stand. My two-year relationship with my boyfriend is very different from his twelve-year legal marriage with his wife. She comes first, and I'm clear on what that entails. When he says that I'm the third most important person in the world to him—next to his wife and daughter—I know that he's speaking the honest truth, and I appreciate that."

Others feel that it creates a hierarchy of love, and some are insulted at being referred to as a secondary, feeling that one ought to love all one's lovers equally. Judie of Wisconsin says, "All my wives are equal in my heart. Learning to love them all equally, without choosing one over the other, has been a wonderful spiritual challenge for me. It's made me grow and stretch as a person. When I find myself feeling less intimate with one of them, I make a point to do something special with her to promote our bond. It's too easy to fall out of love with someone due to a combination of neglect and paying too much attention to another relationship." She concedes, however, that "this only works consistently because we're all polyfidelitous. While I applaud those who want to love all their lovers equally, including ones you only got together with last week, I know that's an awfully difficult thing. If there is a fair way to rank lovers— and on my more idealistic days I don't think that there is—it's about commitment and seniority."

Giovanni of Florida disagreed strongly with the idea that one should strive to love all one's lovers equally. "Maybe it's old-fashioned of me, but the idea that a ten-year marriage should have the same focus and attention and priority as someone you met last month at a gathering, that's insulting. I think that established lovers should set clear expectations of how long someone has to last in a relationship—and what they have to do in order to show a commitment—before they start messing around. My wife's lover had to be around for three years and make a commitment to both of us before we agreed to upgrade her from secondary to another primary. Since she's not romantically involved with me, her commitment to me was as brother to brother, comrade in arms, shared-blood member of the clan. That was important, and it made me able to agree to the promotion."

When it comes to the boundaries themselves, it's pretty easy to see that the power is in the hands of those who set them. Sometimes the primary partners are the ones to set all the boundaries, and sometimes everyone has a certain amount of say. Colleen in Maryland says that "the boundaries are mostly established between my primary and myself, and we then discuss those with our secondaries. They establish boundaries with their primaries and then tell us about them." Others invite anyone who's involved to meet together and work out the boundaries between everyone.

Sometimes lovers move up and down into different slots. When first interviewed, YuleCat of Massachusetts told us that "A and I are primaries in the traditional sense of the word, as well as being married. I have trouble describing my relationship to B, since while not quite primary—I'm married to A, and B is married to someone else—it does have a lot of the depth and intensity of a primary relationship and is not 'secondary' emotionally. However, we have none of the benefits and challenges of living together or running a household together. So she's sort of a 'primary-and-a-half,' though that term isn't really accurate either." Months later, he reported that he and his primary partner had decided to downgrade their relationship to secondaries, although they chose to stay married due to general compatibility.

Contrary to popular belief, not every secondary longs to be a primary. Jen from Boston says, "I enjoy being a secondary. At this stage in my life, I don't have the time or energy to be someone's primary partner . . . In fact, for me, the worst thing about polyamory is the fear, threat, and insecurity I feel when I'm in a polyamorous primary relationship—and that's why I may never have a relationship like that again." Joshua adds, "Right now I'm a secondary for life. I've made a commitment to my sweetheart as my primary, and he's married to his primary partner, which means that I will never be a primary myself. And that's all right, because he's worth it, and because having a poly family is worth it to me."

The issue of polyamory contracts is a much-debated one, similar to the debates surrounding the use of prenuptial contracts. Some polyfolk swear by them; others feel that the use of a written contract is too unromantic or rigid. One poly Pagan reported disliking written contracts because she felt that "having all those things set down in stone makes people less likely to be willing to be flexible when necessary. It's too easy for a contract to become a chain that everyone is afraid to break."

Another wrote in response: "That's nonsense! Of course a contract will need to be renegotiated periodically. That's part of life. Just build in the parameters by which it can be done, and you're fine. After all, we made the thing, we can unmake it."

The following is an example of the polyamory contract that was drawn up between myself and my wife Bella twelve years ago. Although it is a contract for a primary couple who is looking to bring secondaries into their lives, parts of it can be adapted and used for any group of any combination. It's been through a few changes over the years, but for the most part it is the same agreement that we started with. I've exploded it, part by part, with explanations as to why we did what we did, so that you can follow along. It's how the actual mechanics of our relationship work, the Chilton's Guide for our marriage. Let's take a look under the hood and check out the motor and its workings. Maybe by the time I'm done, you'll be able to figure out how to rebuild your own.

Our Polyamory Contract

We, Bella Michelle Kinney Kaldera and Raven Brangwyn Kaldera, do hereby agree to the following rules for our relationship, which can be renegotiated at a future date if both parties are amenable, on a point-by-point basis.

> *Okay, so I've been polyamorous since I've been sexual. At the tender age of fifteen I lost my virginity and realized that there was no way I was going to be able to cope with monogamy, period. If I was told that I couldn't have it, wanting it would drive me crazy. My choices seemed few: cheat on my partners, go through serial monogamous relationships faster than used tissues, live a life entirely of one-night stands, or be polyamorous and work like hell to get it right. Seems like a no-brainer, right?*

1. We affirm that by handfasting, we create a primary relationship. All other relationships will be no more than secondary in priority, regardless of the level of love, lust, and infatuation involved.

> *Being married is really important to me. I didn't realize how important it was until I actually had a well-fitting marriage for the first time. Before, when I'd had relationships—including marriages—that had been a poor fit, I dismissed marriage as something I was doing for the other person, or for society, or for insurance, or whatever. It was when I had something really good that I decided it was worth it to do everything I could not to lose it.*

a) This means that the primary partner will have first claim on the other partner's time, energy, and attention, after such things as childcare, jobs, school, etc.

> *In a monogamous relationship, sex is the coin with which you show the other person how much they are valued. In a polyamorous relationship, where sex is not exclusive, the coin you use instead is time*

and attention. The running joke at our local polyamory support group is that the polyamorous mating call is "Get out your calendars!"

b) This also means that the primary partner's feelings about the situation take priority and are of maximum importance in gauging the viability of a relationship position. Example: If party A and party A's secondary lover(s) think everything is hunky-dory, and party B is upset, party B gets listened to and taken seriously. If one of us thinks something is wrong, something is wrong.

Polyamory is for grownups only. If you can't yet bring yourself to communicate honestly with your partner about everything that goes wrong—and don't wait too long after it goes wrong, and don't lay on guilt when you bring it up—think twice about dragging yet more people in. It might be better to stay monogamous. Polyamory is not the place to work out your neuroses, any more than running a marathon is the best way to exercise your recently broken and healing ankle.

c) We affirm that communication is important, and we promise each other to bring up and discuss reasonably and rationally any feelings of insecurity, abandonment, loneliness, unfairness, etc. as soon as we can articulate them. We agree to take each other's said feelings with the utmost seriousness and not ridicule them. We agree to put constructive suggestions first before paranoia or accusations. We agree to change our behavior whenever necessary with regard to polyamory to make the other partner feel loved and valued.

The key is for every person involved to come at every processing session with a teamwork rather than an oppositional attitude—more like, "We're going to find a way to work this all out together" than "You evil people have hurt me again!"

It's the responsibility of the lover who's feeling hurt to bring it up. It's the responsibility of the others involved to listen and ask how they can make you feel better while not requiring them to feel worse. And, throwing the ball back into the first court, it is the responsibility of the first person to strain their brains and think of something.

d) We also affirm that non-primary lovers are not therapists with which to complain about your primary partners. We request each other to only do such necessary venting with non-sexual friends. Non-primary lovers cannot be used to run messages of pique to the other partner, used as a weapon in an argument when not present to defend themselves, or be put in the middle of a primary-lover argument about an issue other than poly-amory or the relationships involved if they do not wish it.

If you've ever been a secondary lover watching your honey have a knock-down, drag-out with their mate, you know just what an awk-ward and terrifying situation it is. Generally, getting involved makes it worse, no matter how objective you think you are. Even if you are objec-tive, it's unlikely that you'll be perceived that way. Sometimes it's best to take a trip to the corner store for chocolate and let them duke it out.

e) We promise to be honest about our feelings at all times, never to play the martyr in order to look generous, never to dismiss a feeling on the basis of irrationality—all feelings are irrational and will be taken seriously anyway—and never to give in to Shiny New Lover Syndrome, in which infatuation with the new toy precludes attention to the old.

Ah, Shiny New Lover Syndrome, the bane of polyamory! See the sun chapter for help on this one.

2. We agree that although sexual and romantic liaisons with others are permitted, they are permitted only under the following circumstances:

a) If either of us want to have sexual/romantic relations with someone else, they must bring that person in to be interviewed by the other primary partner before sexual relations have occurred.

This is the first place where we weed 'em out. If you're not willing to be grilled by my spouse, then obviously you must not want me that badly, right? Am I worth it or not?

b) The potential lover must affirm that they are fully aware of the situation and have no illusions about the nature of our partnership, including their place in the priority list.

The problem is, of course, that people lie. Another polyamorous couple that we know had a situation like this: he went to a new city 800 miles away to secure his job and find an apartment ahead of time, before she came down with their young child and all their stuff. Once there, he found a new girlfriend, and negotiations were done over the phone. The new girlfriend swore that she understood, but in actuality she was secretly sure that "this polyamory stuff" was just the lead-in to a divorce and that she'd soon be in the wifely place.

Then his wife moved down with their child (and her own girlfriend), and there were no signs of a divorce to be seen. The new girlfriend was mightily disgruntled. Then the husband went out and found himself a new boyfriend and introduced him to the family. At this point the girlfriend realized that they had been telling the truth all along and fled in anguish. It's really hard to tell if someone means it when they smile and say, "Oh, yes, I understand perfectly." Usually I make 'em sign a copy of this contract, saying that they've read and understood it.

c) The potential partner must convince us that they are really polyamorous and not just fooling around between monogamous lovers that they will eventually dump us for. We've been through that too many times.

Actually, it's the single most frequent reason I've been dumped in my entire life. The new lover swears up and down that they are polyamorous, everything goes well for many months, and then they take a new lover who wants them to be monogamous and drop all the other flames. One day you're convinced everything is fine, the next they're telling you goodbye because "This relationship means so much to me, I just have to do it!"

Except that I'd never do that to someone. When I say this is what they can expect, I mean it. If a lover told me I had to be monogamous and dump people with seniority and old, deep connections, I'd tell them to go screw themselves. Really. They knew what they were getting when they took up with me. If they fooled themselves into believing that I wasn't being truthful, that's their stupidity. These days, I tell new lovers up front that if they were ever to do that to me, I will kill them. Verbally, anyway.

In other words, if you're polyamorous, don't date monogamous people and expect it to work out most of the time, no matter how cute they are.

d) The potential lover must be polite and respectful to the other primary partner throughout the relationship.

Hell, yes! At least one of my new lovers was chucked out for being rude to Bella as soon as I was out of the room. You don't have to be my wife's closest friend, or lover, or pal, but you'd better be decent to her and not treat her as if you wish she didn't exist. If you care about me, you will care about the most important person in my life.

e) The potential lover must be okay with kids and not nasty to Raven's daughter. They need not have extensive interactions with her, but they should not regard her as a nuisance or obstacle, at least not where Raven can hear it.

See the moon chapter for advice on kids.

f) No homewrecking. If the potential lover has a partner with any serious level of commitment (e.g., from regular boyfriend/girlfriend to spouse), that partner must speak to both of us and give his/her blessing to the idea. If they are less than okay with it, the lover is disqualified. Anyone lying about not having such a level of commitment, when in actuality they do, will immediately be disqualified on the spot upon discovery. Loud scenes are appropriate at this time.

This is an especially important one. You do not want to be in the middle of some couple's marital problems. I don't care how much you want a married person whose significant other is demanding monogamy; cheating is wrong. Lying to one's significant other and/or encouraging someone else to do so is wrong. Obviously, folks like this have things to work out; tell them that they have to do their homework before they get to play. Always take the moral high ground. It's better than having an angry significant other coming after you with an ax. If they can't give you their blessing, get out of there before it blows up in your face.

g) Each primary partner has the right to an irrevocable veto of any partner at any time. On the first interview, the vetoer is required to provide an explanation, but the veto is not open to argument. If an already long-standing sex partner is suddenly vetoed, arguing is allowed and a consensus must be reached.

Part of real love is being able to say to your lover, "I trust you with control over who I sleep with, because I trust you to make your decision based not on your own insecurities but on a real consideration of my needs, wishes, and safety." If you do not have this level of trust in them, you need to pull back from polyamorous adventures and work on trust building within the relationship.

h) Any and all emotional misunderstandings must be settled by consensus, with mediation if necessary, before they become resentful and blow up. Repeated inability on the part of non-primary lovers to talk through misunderstandings and come to useful compromises will result in disqualification due to immaturity. Repeated unwillingness to bring up emotional resentments before they become dangerous will have the same result. Inability to get along with other primary partners after repeated processing will also have the same result. Remember, the committed relationship comes first.

In order to consent to a lover's liaison, you must first feel secure in the relationship. The other part of love, the reply to the above quote, is: "I can consent to these other relationships because I trust you to take my emotional needs into consideration, to be clear about what position I hold in your life, and to respond immediately when I am feeling insecure."

i) If genetic male-identified males wish to date Bella, they must first court Raven's permission to do so. Gifts are encouraged.

This is a negotiation around possessiveness and insecurities that we are both especially proud of. When it came to Bella seeing other people, somehow it was very hard for me when she wanted to see genetic male-identified males. I worried that she'd revert to a former pattern of being attracted to abusive, alcoholic jerks. I worried that they'd treat me politely on the surface, but inside they'd be laughing at me for letting them "screw my woman." I worried that they'd start pissing contests with me out of sheer habit. And, yes, I was just kind of possessive and insecure.

However, Bella, like me, is bisexual, and didn't want her activities curtailed in ways I wasn't willing to curtail mine. So it was my responsibility to figure out how to solve the problem: under what circumstances could a theoretical guy date my wife without getting my hackles up? What would he have to do to make me feel good about it? The solution that I finally came up with was that they would have to court me for permission to be with her—give me gifts, or take me out male-bonding, or otherwise make the effort to show that they respected me and cared enough about her to go through that process.

When her ex-lover came back into her life (as he often does between monogamous girlfriends, a situation that would drive me mad but that she doesn't mind), he dropped off a spare motorcycle that an ex-roommate had given him. "It needs some work, and I don't have the time to fix it. Do you want it?" What could I do but grin and say, "Go have fun!"

j) Although secondary lovers do not have to have a separate friend-type relationship with the other primary partner, in which they spend time just with them, it is a definite bonus and likely to earn them favor. This should be suggested to them.

Frankly, if they can't be at least some kind of friends, do you really want to be in the middle of that, possibly for years?

3. There are restrictions on the following social activities:

a) The following nights must be spent with the primary partner: Anniversaries. Birthdays and rebirthdays. The eight religious high holidays of our church. Graduations and any other days of special emotional significance. As soon as one partner falls asleep, however, the duty is considered fulfilled.

This is where priorities come in, right? When one lover's black belt competition falls on the other lover's birthday, you'd better start negotiating well in advance. I highly recommend having calendars that you all compare and adjust regularly. In fact, don't come to a processing session without them.

b) Only primary partners can play spouses in historical recreation games.

This works for us, because it happens to be a hobby we do together. Obviously, if Bella hated that sort of thing and another one of my lovers liked it, this would be different. It's one of the great things about polyamory—no matter what the event or interest, you can probably find someone willing to escort you there. The problem comes when they all want to go, and who gets to decorate your arm? Talk it out beforehand.

c) Use of the words "wife," "husband," and "spouse" are restricted to the primary partnership only. "Partner" is acceptable only for live-in primaries and secondaries. Other words, such as "boyfriend," "girlfriend," "lover," "fuckbuddy," etc., are fine for other contacts.

I currently have one wife, one boyfriend, and one fuckbuddy. That's how they each prefer to be referred to. Words are very powerful and have strong connotations. It's worth it to get your titles right.

4. There are restrictions on the following sexual activities:

a) Body-fluid monogamy at all times with non-primary lovers. This means latex. Exceptions for individuals who have been lovers for at least six months with both primary partners and who are willing to do body-fluid monogamy with all other lovers, can be negotiated.

This is very important to us, not just for emotional reasons but for our physical safety. If you are not going to be monogamous, you have to work three times as hard to be safe out there in the world of communicable diseases. I once dumped, quite painfully and with a lot of tears, a former primary partner who went to a gathering, had unsafe sex, came home, and had unsafe sex with me before relating the extent of the previous adventures. I'm sorry, but this is unforgivable. It shows that you don't care about your partner's life, much less your own.

b) Bella will experience penetrative sex only with Raven.

Sometimes it's a good thing to have one special sexual act, even above and beyond those acts limited by body-fluid monogamy, that is only for primary partners. It means that when you do this one thing, you are affirming your unique relationship to each other; that it is irreplaceable and unlike any other connection in your lives. It's okay to have one special thing for each relationship, of course, but it's best to pick things that aren't the other partner's cup of tea anyway, if possible.

c) If BDSM is going to be happening, the primary partner has the right to demand to be present in order to make sure the other partner will be safe. Each person's discretion.

We do BDSM, which makes things a little more complicated. Bringing leathersex into a relationship means extra negotiating—like several hours' worth. Even little things—"If I call you Sir, do I have to call her Ma'am even if I'm not lovers with her?" "Er . . . have you actually ever done it with that thing in reality?" can present problems if not worked out first.

d) Beds are first and foremost for sleeping in. If loud sex in the big bed between a primary and secondary lover is keeping the other primary lover awake, they have the power of eviction.

There's nothing so pissy in the morning as a partner who was kept awake all night listening to you have sex. Even if they didn't really want to be involved in it, but just wanted to sleep. Actually, especially if they just wanted to sleep. Be considerate.

5. *Hunting licenses.* If one partner is going away on a trip and wants to be able to take advantage of sexual contacts during that time when interviewing is not available, s/he can apply to the other partner for a "hunting license." This will entail the license holder to have sex without prior interviewing or permission. Rules pertaining:

a) Hunting licenses do not have to be granted. Their refusal need not be explained and cannot be argued. They are a privilege, not a right.

We borrowed the term "hunting license" from another polyamorous couple. All negotiating aside, sometimes there will be times when you're by yourself in a faraway place and just can't get the other partner on the phone. By limiting the possibility of such out-of-left-field encounters to times when it's expected, you cut down on insecurity. Granted, if your partner is feeling insecure and doesn't want to grant you one, it's hard to be good about it, but you have to keep telling yourself that this relationship is worth more than any possible quickie. There will be other quickies. Years of love are hard to replace.

b) They are only good for the specified period of time.

c) Sexual contacts picked up on a hunting license can only be one-shot deals. If, after returning home, once the license has expired, the partner wants to continue to see this contact, they must start from scratch as if there had been no sex, bringing them for a standard interview. All rules and vetoes then apply.

d) The sexual contacts during the licensing period must be made fully aware of the polyamorous situation, including what they can expect afterwards, and must not have significant others who would object. (This must be verified with a phone call.)

I don't know how many times I've been in negotiation with someone I've just met whose significant other is "totally okay with them doing it with other people," and when I ask to call the significant other and make sure of this fact, they turn pale and suddenly aren't quite so interested in me anymore. Hmmm. Funny, that.

e) The first free time directly following the cessation of a hunting license period must be spent in quality time with the primary partner.

Ah, crawling back into bed with the body that you know and love so well! I definitely find that absence makes the heart—and the loins—grow fonder. There's something wonderful to knowing that you can have your cake and eat it too, with a little work on the sidelines. It's also wonderful to know that the love between you is so big that it doesn't have to be kept confined in a tiny box. Well, all right, maybe this contract is just our way of putting it in a much bigger box, a playground, a stage, so that it won't get lost or dissipated. Boundaries are good. They tell you just how much—exactly how much—you are loved.

We hereby agree to abide by the rules of this contract until it is renegotiated, or until we die, or until the world ends.

—RAVEN AND BELLA KALDERA

Many Hands of Love:
A Polyamorous Handfasting Rite

This ritual was originally published in *Handfasting and Wedding Rituals: Inviting Hera's Blessing* (Llewellyn, 2003), but I am reprinting it here as a resource. In order to make this ritual as flexible as possible, it's been designed with interchangeable parts. The opening and closing are used with all the variations; the middle section with the vows has two different versions, of which one may hopefully fit your group of lovers.

Everyone stands in the boundary of the circle, with the lovers next to the officiant. The callers of the four quarters should have either long scarves that they can wave about, or ribbons tied to sticks, or something else that flows through the air. They recite their invocation facing the direction of their element, and then they walk (or run, or skip, or dance) around the entirety of the circle, waving their fabric to sweep away negative influences, returning to the direction in which they began. Each caller waits until the last one has completed the circle before beginning their invocation.

> East: *I call the Great Winds of Change*
>
> *And the Words of Power!*
>
> *May language spring forth*
>
> *And never be thwarted!*
>
> *May clarity spring forth*
>
> *And never be muddied!*
>
> *May honesty spring forth*
>
> *And never be suppressed!*
>
> *May all the hateful words of the past*
>
> *Be blown clean away!*

South: *I call the Great Flame of Passion*

And the Hearth of Power!

May heat rise between bodies

Like a volcano!

May love burn strong

And never die out!

May inspiration spark

And bloom into manifestation!

May all the smoldering anger of the past

Be burned clean away!

West: *I call the Great Ocean of Feeling*

And the River of Power!

May tenderness flow forth

And never be scorned!

May compassion flow forth

And never be slighted!

May joy flow like water

And never be dammed!

May all the old jealousies of the past

Be washed clean away!

North: *I call upon the Great Stone of Enduring*

And the Mountain of Power!

May patience grow

And never be stunted!

May caring grow

And be well tended!

May laughter be seeded

And joy grow from its sprouting!

May all the old assumptions be but fertilizer

To grow a new kind of love in a clean ground!

Officiant: We call upon Aphrodite, goddess of love and beauty, on this day of celebrating love. We call especially on her aspect of Aphrodite Urania, builder of bridges, joiner of hands across incalculable abysses, she who brings together. Lady of Love Unexpected but always welcome. Your presence shows us that there can never be too much love in the world. We call also upon her son Eros, the will to love that cannot be overcome or underestimated. Lord of Love Irresistible, your presence shows us that no matter what anyone says, love cannot be denied. And you, _____ and _____ and _____ and _____ *(speak first names of lovers),* do you all come here of your own free will to join in the bonds of love?

Lovers: We do!

Version 1

For the next part, we have two alternate versions. This first version is for a primary couple relationship where one person is adding a new lover who will not necessarily be lovers with the other spouse. The officiant should have two cords, one golden and one silver.

Officiant: You, _____ and _____ *(naming primary partners),* have been committed to each other for some time now. We here honor that bond by showing it to all. *(Officiant ties their hands together with the golden cord.)* Many blessings be on your love, and may it be the solid ground from which each of you fly.

Partner 1: Our love is strong and solid, and nothing can change it. Any addition to our family will only add love, not subtract it.

Partner 2: Our love is stable and constant, and nothing can lessen it. Any addition to our family will simply add to our commitment.

Partner 1: I love you now and for always.

Partner 2: I love you now and for always.

Officiant: Now you have come to a new voyage of discovery. _____ has found great love with _____ *(third partner)* and wishes to be bound in marriage with her/him as well. Speak now your love with pride!

Partner 2: (speaks about how s/he met the third partner, and what love has grown between them, and speaks of new beginnings, and then says:) I would bring you into the circle of love that is my family, for there is no reason to break and part what can be shared with more joy.

Partner 3: (speaks about how s/he loves the second partner, and how s/he sees this new family, and speaks of new beginnings, and then says:) I will gladly come into the circle of love that is your family, and I wish to bring it still more love and joy. *(They take hands, and the officiant binds the silver cord around their hands, so that the second partner is bound on both sides.)*

Partner 2: I love you now and for always.

Partner 3: I love you now and for always.

Partner 1 (to partner 3): I swear to be a sister (or brother) to you, _____, and I swear always to believe in your love for me, _____, and I swear to never let fear and insecurity override the goodness that I know is here in this circle.

Partner 3 (to partner 1): I swear to be a sister (or brother) to you, _____, and I swear always to believe in your love for me, _____, and I swear to never let fear and insecurity override the goodness that I know is here in this circle.

Partner 2: I will be your friend now and for always.

Partner 3: I will be your friend now and for always.

Version 2

This next version can be used for a handfasting where three or more people are handfasted all together. We have used an example of four, but this ritual can be expanded or contracted to any number of people. The quarters are called, and the officiant speaks as above.

Each lover stands forward and presents his or her cord. It should be twelve feet long, with knots tied at specific places that correspond to the following measurements: their height, the width from fingertip to fingertip when the arms are outstretched, the diameter of the chest encircling the heart, and the diameter of the head around the forehead. Although they will be in different colors, chosen by each lover to symbolize themselves, they should all be about the same thickness. Each cord should be marked in some way with some bodily fluid of the person who has knotted it. (This is the classic witch's measure.)

Officiant: In elder days, when witches would meet in a coven at night, their lives depended upon secrecy. The coven elders would take their measure with a cord, and use this against them if need be. Today, however, we live in happier times, where we can practice openly both our faith and our different ways of loving, and each of these lovers has brought with them their measure, as a gift and not a hostage, to offer up to this marriage in the name of love. Come forth, you who love and would be bound in love, and show the gifts of yourselves that you bring.

The following are examples of possible things to say, in order to inspire you to create your own lines.

Partner 1: My cord is green, symbolizing growth. I bring to this marriage the ability to grow and change, and to help my lovers also to grow and change, and to always see the new green of spring in the frost of each passing winter.

Partner 2: My cord is red, symbolizing passion. I bring to this marriage my intensity. I will passionately love and defend this marriage and everyone in it, and I will never let things become dull and flat and boring.

Partner 3: My cord is silver, symbolizing communication. I bring to this marriage an almost unlimited ability to talk, and process, and keep the lines of communication open. I will never let there be unsaid words that create resentments or secret pain.

Partner 4: My cord is brown, symbolizing work and loyalty. I bring to this marriage the ability to keep going in spite of hard times, to remain faithful and be patient, and to work hard at whatever I can do to make things better for us.

Officiant: Place your cords together, end to end, and each take a turn knotting them together at one end.

Partner 1: By this first knot, I honor our new beginnings.

Partner 2: By this second knot, I honor the path we walk together.

Partner 3: By this third knot, I honor the future we face together.

Partner 4: By this fourth knot, I honor the love we share.

Officiant: Now I will hold the end of this cord, as the gods hold firmly the silver cord of your souls in place on this Earth. You will all do the work of braiding these separate cords into one. *(They begin to braid. This may take a while. During this, the circle of people may drum, or chant, or sing. At the end, they tie the final knot all together. The officiant takes the braided cord. Then each lover places their right hand into the center of the circle, and the officiant wraps the braided rope around their hands.)* You are now bound each to all, each with all, each by all. Each strand alone may be broken, but together they are truly unbreakable.

At this point, the two alternate versions merge, and the officiant continues the same for both.

Officiant: Each lover that you have had in the past has enriched your life with the experience of their love. You bring that wealth to this handfasting. Use it wisely, taking the best as an example but not allowing the worst to stop you in your tracks. It takes many hands to carry a great love. Grasp this love with both hands and do not hold back. This handfasting will not lie easy in the eyes of many people. Some will raise their voices against you and your choices. Do you swear to close your ears to their doubt and hear only the love and support of your chosen family?

Lovers: We do!

Officiant: Do you swear to be considerate of one another, to be patient with one another, and to see as often as possible the divine spirit within each other?

Lovers: We do!

Officiant: Do you swear to hold strong to your love, to not be swayed by hard times, and yet always make every effort to ensure the happiness of every partner in this circle?

Lovers: We do!

Officiant: Do you swear to work through jealousy, and insecurity, and fear, and do what is necessary to appease all inner demons, no matter how hard the path?

Lovers: We do!

Officiant (to all present): I ask all present, all witnesses, to stand and answer this question: Do you all here swear to honor the love and the handfasting of these your friends, no matter what the voices of others say?

All Present: We do!

Officiant: I then declare you all handfast in the eyes of the gods, in the name of Aphrodite Urania, and the archer Eros. May love and joy be your constant companions and lie in your beds with you every night. Good fortune to a new-formed family! You may now embrace and kiss.

Lovers kiss, and the rite is ended.

Till Death Do Us All Part

Of course, the strongest boundary of all is death, also ruled by Saturn. Death is something that few people like to think about when they contemplate starting a relationship, but if it does last until old age there is a certainty that death will become an issue. Sometimes it visits before old age, taking people by surprise and unprepared.

More than once I have attended the funeral of a polyamorous person where two lovers were present, but only one was acknowledged to the onlooking family and friends who didn't know about the deceased person's lifestyle. In these cases, we found that our primary duty was to aid the other lover in whatever way we could, supporting their right to grief.

When I interviewed poly Pagans, I found that very few of them had put together wills or other legal documentation that provided for their polyamorous lovers in the event of someone's death. Of the few who had done so, most had children to deal with, a situation that makes most people more motivated to do something about their eventual demise. Even if you don't have children, however, do think about the emotional health of your lovers should you pass on. Are they likely to fight among each other, for whatever reason, regarding what should be done about your funeral arrangements and the dispersion of your possessions? If so, make your will very clear on the matter, and ask them ahead of time to respect it.

If you have time to plan for a reasonably imminent death—and if you are elderly, that's not as unlikely a thing as most younger people might think—think about who you want to see supported at your funeral and in the days following your passing. If one of your lovers is likely to get less support than another—or even, for that matter, scorn and opprobrium from unsympathetic friends or family—make sure that you have sympathetic friends designated to give them support and defend them when the time comes.

I've seen emotionally raw issues around polyamory arise many times at polyamorous funerals; in fact, I can't think of one where I didn't see any. Usually it's people who want to rewrite history and pretend that the deceased wasn't poly or who think that now that they're dead, their "misguided errors" can simply be ignored. Some people even blame the surviving partners. One member of a polyamorous triad that I know committed suicide after many years of unsuccessfully fighting depression. His wife and her partner, after years of trying to keep him afloat and helping him through one failed course of therapy after another, were blamed by many members of their community for the suicide—of course, it was reasoned, he killed himself because he couldn't come to terms with the fact that his wife had been sleeping with another man for several years. One angry individual even told their young son that his mother's relationship with her boyfriend had killed his father.

One polyamorous woman, who chose to remain anonymous, upon discovering the cancer that eventually killed her worried that there would be recriminations and accusations toward her two secondary lovers after her death. She wrote not only a will but a long poem, which I am fortunate enough to be able to reproduce here. It was read at her funeral, and copies of it were given to everyone who attended and sent to those who could not come. It left no questions as to the nature of her lovestyle, and her lovers, and their devotion.

(All names have been changed. If you know the individuals involved, please respect their privacy and do not print their names.)

TERRY'S HEART

If you are hearing this poem spoken
By any other tongue but mine,
I am going into the ground before your eyes.

If you are reading these words I have written,
And I am not standing before you,
My eyes pleading for your acceptance,
Then I am lying before you
Waiting to become one with the earth.
My spirit is long fled

Or perhaps I hover over you, loving, worried,

Hoping that my death will not be merely

More misery for those who love me.

Know that I welcome Death, that She

Is a kinder lover than her sister, Pain,

The hungry bride who has shared my bed these many years.

Her clawing fingers ate at my aching body

And only three things held her back,

Three hearts, three bodies, three minds

That worked in tandem, tirelessly, to win me back from her

Inch by inch, until sweet Death could take her place.

I name and praise them, my litany

Of all that is good in the world.

I name you, Jerry, deftest hand with needles,

Baker of weedy brownies, changer of bandages.

I heard you weep as you put food through the blender

For me, searching always for the perfect potion

That would slip itself past my nausea.

You delivered them to me with a flourish

And a smile to cover your red eyes.

Giver of hour-long footrubs, scrubber of floors,

I know that you picked out the clothes

That wrap my husk as I go down.

I name you, Rike, reader of poetry,

Who read me books till you were hoarse

When my eyes went, even though you hated politics

And romance novels, which were loves of mine.

Long tall woman who cut off your hair

In solidarity, when I lost mine.

Your braid is wrapped around my wrist now,

As you said it would be, and I believe you

Because you always kept your word.

Your shorn locks, entwined with mine,

Will be my passport past the river of tears.

And finally, I name you, Duncan,

Great bear of the northern sky,

Strong arms that lifted me,

Gentle hands that cleansed me,

Silent patience that walked me down the road,

Step by step, to the bitter end.

I cannot count the times I cried

And you stood strong; I can only fear,

As I hover here above you,

That I could not, in my weakness, give back that comfort.

May your strength bring me back

To the gate of rebirth, the Mother's womb,

Like a memory of eternity.

My beloveds, my heart is divided among you,

Not like a house divided, but like a feast,

Like a jug of wine or a loaf of bread,

Shared between the worthy. I will be the bond

Between you, even as you go your ways.

Terry's heart is yours, as your bodies were mine,

Cradling me in the dark, one by one,

Keeping me in light until that light faded,

Keeping me in warmth until I cooled,

Keeping me in love until I believed

That love could live on past death,

Keeping me anchored until I could let go.

I praise your names, my three beacons,

And let everyone who hears my song

Praise you as well, with the highest praise

For your courage, your devotion,

And your eternally bright souls.

PART V

Spirit

*What's All This Got to Do
with Pagan Religion Anyway?*

In the traditional symbolism of the pentagram, the four lower points stand for the four elements, and the fifth point is the place of spirit, the soul-force that binds them all together. Few relationships travel to this point. Most spend so much time in the embodied elements—talking, balancing power, dealing with feelings and practical matters—that the spiritual aspect of the relationship is rarely experienced. It's even more rare when the people involved get to the point of dealing with how their relationship affects the spiritual atmosphere of a community or of the world.

This is the question on which this book turns. Up until this point, I've viewed Pagan polyamorous relationships in purely personal and practical terms. At this point, where the personal becomes communal, I will shift the focus to how polyamory fits in with the community spiritual views of the Pagan demographic.

About a third of the polyamorous Pagans I interviewed felt that their choice to be polyamorous had nothing whatsoever to do with their choice of religion. Some were poly before they came to Paganism. However, of the ones who came to it afterward, most admitted that they saw their first positive examples of it in the Pagan community and often hooked up with their first poly partners there. The Pagan demographic—and especially Pagan festivals—have become something of a temporary "dating pool" for polyamorous people.

Others felt that although their religion and their lifestyle were separate, both reflected a particular mindset that attracted them. Galadriel in Philadelphia writes: "I'm poly and I'm Pagan. I'm not poly because I'm Pagan. I believe I'm poly because I have a different view about the nature of relationships, and I think this supports my views on Paganism as well. Such as: 1) Love is the only infinite resource.

2) To share love is never wrong. 3) We are not separate from each other or any other existing thing." She adds that "polyamory is just another offshoot of having an open mind and questioning social norms. It's about freedom."

A large majority felt that tolerant Pagan sexual morals lent themselves well to polyamory, or, for that matter, any sexual lifestyle between consenting adults. In fact, of the folks who were polyamorous before coming to Paganism, most did admit that one of the most attractive things about this religion was the sexual tolerance for many different lifestyles, including polyamory. One triad commented, "Our Pagan and poly beliefs both reflect a greater flexibility with regard to our outlooks. We are big supporters of 'live and let live,' because that is what we want for ourselves."

"I feel that Paganism is a path which can support and nurture all types of relationship structures, from poly, monogamy, celibate or platonic, BDSM, whatever," says Jen from Boston. "Socially, the current Pagan community around here seems to be very accepting of different lovestyles. Ethically speaking, it's a little trickier, because Neopaganism does not have a well-defined set of ethics. But most of the poly Pagans I know go out of their way to be open, honest, to care about their partner's feelings, and so forth. Morally, as long as it harms none, it's all good. Culturally, I think that at this point polyamory has become part of Neopagan culture . . . to the extent that I have heard monogamous people are starting to feel excluded or pressured. That's kind of funny in an ironic sort of way, but still not a good thing. Cosmologically? All acts of love and pleasure are her rituals. 'Nuff said."

WG from Boston agrees: "Having deeply committed relationships on a physical as well as an emotional level are part of the celebration of the life that blesses us. Polyamory is completely in accordance with the Charge of the Goddess, and it makes many, many people very happy. And it can and does work. Love is never wrong."

Giovanni from Florida enthuses: "Diversity! It's all about diversity! In our faith, as opposed to many other people's beliefs, diversity is not only good, it's sacred. This is a nature religion . . . and look at nature! Many, many different kinds of relationships bonding, sometimes in pairs, sometimes in groups. Mating differences within species as well as between species. As a scientist, I can't pretend that I'm not part of that big diverse biological community. The bonobos [pygmy chimpanzees] to whom we are most closely related—who but for 5 percent of their genes would be us—have polyamorous group relations that use group sex to soothe communal tension. I'm not saying that the natural thing is for us all to act like bonobos, but that if we really believe that nature is sacred and worth looking to for our philosophy of life, then we must admit that there are many diverse ways for human beings to form love bonds. To do otherwise would be to set us apart from the natural order of things, and as a Pagan and a scientist, I can't do that."

Judie from Wisconsin had a more heartfelt appeal: "As a Pagan, I am both a polytheist and a pantheist. I am also a goddess worshipper. That means that I love and worship many goddesses, while still understanding that everyone and everything comes from the same source, the universal womb of Love and Life. In dealing with my lovers, I use the example of the Goddess from whose womb all things spring. She loves all her creations equally and unconditionally. I'm only one woman, but I can still strive for that kind of love, if only between three other people. If she can love all of creation equally, I can love three wives equally."

She speaks eloquently of the links between her Pagan faith and her practice of polyamory: "On the other side, I am not dedicated to one goddess alone. Sometimes I revere Artemis, with her independence and dedication; sometimes I revere Demeter, who nurtures with passion; sometimes I revere Brigid, who is all fire and creativity. They are all worthy of my attention. And in my daily life, I love Anatolia, who is unswerving in her loyalty to her marriage, her daughter, and her politics; Sondra, who is quiet and reflective and can guess what her wives are thinking when they weep; and Brenna, who sings and plays the fiddle and sewed frogs on my jean pockets. Their bodies are the altars at which I worship them, just as I would light a candle first for Artemis and then for Demeter without worrying about whether I am being faithful. Monotheism and monogamy: both are too limiting for me to learn to love fully in the best way for me."

Of course, not all Pagans marry other Pagans, polyamorously or otherwise. About half of the people that we interviewed had non-Pagan primary partners, and around three-quarters had other non-Pagan partners. In any relationship between Pagans and non-Pagans, one of the biggest problems seems to be the issue of differing sexual values. Some of the respondents bemoaned the fact that Paganism had opened them up to being more sex-positive, but they were unable to budge the opinions of partners who still saw sex as something vaguely obscene, or at least profane rather than sacred. One respondent broke up with her long-term partner over the clash of Pagan versus non-Pagan sexual values, even though both were doing fine at polyamory. "I discovered that sexuality was sacred," she lamented, "and then I discovered that I couldn't bring myself to have sex with someone who was determined to see it as naughty and bad, even if that made it more exciting for them."

Shanna in Arizona tells of the issues around dealing with an interfaith poly relationship. "My husband's father was of Jewish extraction, and his mother was raised Mormon, so he says that he comes to a long tradition of polygamy on both sides. He was able to see the usefulness of polyamory easily enough, although he doesn't talk about it at the synagogue that he attends with his father's family. The problem comes when he's exposed to the Neopagan subculture, which he dislikes—he thinks that they're a bunch of indiscriminate hippies. It's taken me a while to get him to come to a gathering—not because I want to convert him, which would be insulting and impossible, but because I want him to see that my spiritual practices are not dangerous or immoral. He finally came to one and did say that it didn't look too bad, although that might be because he spent practically the whole weekend in the hot tub."

Sometimes, even if all the partners are Pagan-inclined, the level of experience can be an issue, especially if the other partner(s) brought the person into Paganism. Wintersong, Fireheart, and Summerwind, a triad in Massachusetts, explain: "Summerwind came to Paganism and magic much later in life than Fireheart (who was raised Pagan and practicing magic) or Wintersong (who began practicing magic and Paganism behind his parents' backs at thirteen). As a result, part of our relationship has been centered around teaching Summerwind about Paganism and magic, which is a significant part of our lives . . . Bringing Summerwind up to speed on what Fireheart and Wintersong have learned has been a long and at times difficult process, which we had to work very hard to keep from affecting the personal side of our relationship."

Other differences between even an all-Pagan set of lovers can crop up. There may be disagreements over which gatherings to attend with whom or what magical practices are appropriate. The Massachusetts triad also recounts that their biggest source of religious disagreement was "how much interaction we wanted within the broader Pagan demographic. We have found that disagreements in our religious, spiritual, and magical lives need to be handled like any other important disagreement that we have. This means we discuss (sometimes at high volume) and eventually compromise (which usually leaves us all equally displeased). Lastly, and most importantly, when one of us comes around, we try very hard not to gloat. Generally we've found that, especially with our spiritual lives, compromising in order to try something new (like attending a ritual with a different group of people) almost always leads to a resolution. Either the person agreeing to do something will like it after all and we will all be happy, or they won't and we all have to stop and reassess the situation."

Although most of the Pagans interviewed were vehement that they didn't pressure their lovers into practicing Pagan religion, a good many of them reported secondary lovers who got curious, got interested, and then got involved, largely due to their pleasure at finding a religion that didn't penalize them for being polyamorous. Others were faced with it from walking into poly families that were also functioning magical or worship groups. YuleCat in Massachusetts comments that "my secondary lover, much to my surprise, suddenly wanted to attend a Samhain ritual that a mutual friend of ours was running about a year and a half ago. I already knew that she was open-minded, as she came out of the science fiction convention scene. She could feel the energy we were raising just as well as any of the rest of us. I think it was probably this particular ritual that started her leaning toward Paganism in the first place."

Not all Pagans practice magic, but of the respondents who made it a major part of their Pagan practices, most had done or regularly did magic with their lovers as a group. Rachel in Florida reports that "Giovanni and I never did magic together, because he felt that he wouldn't be good at it, that it was a 'woman's thing' that men just didn't have a knack for. The male magicians that he'd met all seemed to have a very ceremonial approach that he didn't like at all. When JT came into my life, she was already doing folky magic, but she came at it from a very tribal perspective—making sacred space with a hand-rolled herbal cigarette, putting mojo on the chains on her boots, getting ritual tattoos, stuff like that. No candles and fancy incense, just a stripped-down kind of urban folk magic. Gio immediately took to her way of doing things—actually, it was one of the bonds between them as friends—and they started pressuring me to do things in a less 'fluffy,' feminine way so that we could all work together. I've had to learn a new magical aesthetic, which was difficult for me. I like spending two hours building a fancy altar and having all the goddess figures and everything! But now I do that for my personal spells, and I work with their magical style when we need to do magic together. We ritually clean the house on the solstices and equinoxes, we do money spells, and other stuff. I tried to join a coven once, but there wasn't the intimacy of doing it with people whose bodies and minds you know. So I suppose you could say that they are my coven, along with a close friend who often comes over and helps with the magic. Polyamory created my magical working group."

Judie in Wisconsin also spoke of magical working as a family grouping: "We do two kinds of group magic: sex magic and nonsexual magic. The latter category comes into play for kitchen-blessing spells, lost-cat-finding spells, things like that. We've been working together for so long that we each have parts to play. Brenna and Sondra can sing, so they add the musical element that ties everything together, even if it's only humming in harmony. Anatolia is the best energy-mover by far, and she's got the will that can just push the rest of our wills right up through that cone of power and out. My job is 'coloring' the energy with our needs, as I'm the best visualizer. We do these spells touching, always, if only aura to aura. When we touch in a circle, we create a circuit, and we know exactly what to do . . . Sex magic is saved for either worship or serious emergency magic."

The Tashlins in Massachusetts have turned their polyamorous family into a three-person teaching coven that takes in students for magical training. They also work together as magical partners: "From the beginning, we had intended this to be a working as well as a romantic relationship. We do workings in which we each fill in a position or role, or in which two of us only provided energy or grounding for the third, who performs the actual spell or energy work, as well as all three of us working together to fill one position (such as 'corner guardian'). We've tried to ensure that we all share a common set of basic skills, so that when we work with other people we can be as interchangeable as possible in a basic magical or ritual context. That said, however, we each certainly have individual strengths and weaknesses that we work with or around in our private practice. For instance, Fireheart and Wintersong are both highly skilled in magical cleansing and protection, and they are superior fighters. Summerwind is a better analytical scholar than either of them and is better at making connections between different magical traditions. Fireheart is better at rune divinations and herbs, but Wintersong has a closer working relationship with the gods and is a better healer. And so on."

As Pagan teachers, they have found that having an intimately connected "teaching staff" is a useful thing: "The way in which Tashlin magic is taught is very one-on-one focused, although students eventually work with all of us. Having only one teacher at a time prevents the feeling of being ganged up on . . . but that's not to say that we have not at times taken advantage of that phenomenon to double-team an especially difficult student. More often, we have been known to have one of us ridden or spoken through by a spirit-teacher or god, while another one of us represents Tashlin's interests and opinions on a student's situation . . . We've had to learn to discuss our differing perspectives and opinions on a student's progress in private, since what we see as a discussion of two or three views on the same issue or technique may be seen as a disagreement by a student, which has the potential to pit one teacher against the other in their minds."

Pagan organizations vary in their acceptance of polyamory. Nearly all seem to be at least lip-service tolerant of it, although some may be made more uncomfortable when sizeable numbers of people in their group begin experimenting with it. "Some of these covens and groups make a lot of noise about the 'all acts of love and pleasure' law," one polyamorous Pagan sulked, "but when you actually bring in your girlfriend and boyfriend, they get weird at you." Other groups are not only tolerant but appreciative of polyamorous family bonds. "It has a lot to do with whether or not the leaders of the group are or have been polyamorous," another Pagan commented wryly. "It's worse, actually, if they tried it and it went terribly wrong. I've seen survivors of a bad poly experiment have the most suspicious attitude of all toward it."

Of all Pagan organizations, the Church of All Worlds (CAW) is the most openly pro-polyamory sect. As documented in Margot Adler's classic tome *Drawing Down the Moon*, CAW was originally based on the science fiction novel *Stranger in a Strange Land* by Robert Heinlein. Oberon Zell-Ravenheart, one of the founders of CAW, describes the situation as "many, if not most (although not all) CAW Waterkin are polyamorous. This is one of the main attractions bringing people to CAW in the first place. CAW may be the only legal church in the world that openly and publicly supports polyamory, performs marriage rites for multiples, etc. Throughout the 1960s and up to the present, CAW was a pioneer in creating sustainable communities ('Nests') based on open polyamorous relationships. Numerous long-term, committed, caring, multiple-partner families and communities became well-established throughout the United States and Australia, in which varying degrees of sexual relationships among the members were a glue binding these communities together. One of the most important elements of these relationships was that all the lovers were known to each other and deeply involved in each others' lives on many levels."

Other Pagan groups vary in their acceptance of polyamory. Some covens and groups and churches may tolerate it; others may disapprove, depending on the "group cultural climate" in any given group. Most large groups will have a policy of tolerance for all minorities firmly in place, but whether that manifests as grudging or openhearted tolerance will vary from group to group, and it's impossible to tell until you've been in one. In general, the Pagan groups most likely to enthusiastically welcome it are those with already extant long-term polyamorous members and also those with a significant number of sexual and gender-identified minorities in their group. My own Pagan tradition, Asphodel, is made up of approximately 50 percent from members of sexual, gender, and relationship minority groups, and as such polyamory is considered a perfectly valid alternative. The high concentration of these minority members does reflect their tendency to gravitate to a place where they will be accepted.

It also reflects the tendency of Pagans who are uncomfortable at being in a group where their preferences are not in the overwhelming majority to be unwilling to join. Some people are able to be tolerant of one or two anomalies, but when they're surrounded by them, they feel threatened. In coming into a Pagan group that seems unsure of how to deal with your polyamorous relationship, it may be wise to take some time and think about how you will get certain crucial messages across. These messages would be:

1. That you are not proselytizing for polyamory; i.e., that you don't think of yourself as a more enlightened person just because you have an "alternative lifestyle" or that polyamory is necessarily more "evolved" than monogamy. If you do feel this way, perhaps you should be looking for a more obviously "alternative" group.

2. That you are not coming to this group to cruise for prospective partners. This is the first worry that many coupled individuals have, especially if their partnerships are shaky. It may even be worth your while to let it be known that you don't think it's a good idea to get sexually involved with anyone in a new group during the "tryout period."

3. That just because you are polyamorous does not mean that you are sexually indiscriminate and would engage in relations with anyone who asks. If this is actually your sexual path, you should probably be looking for a group that openly honors their sacred sluts, rather than trying to hide this from other group members, who will likely find out anyway.

4. That just because you are polyamorous does not mean that you do not respect the committed bonds of others and their feelings about those bonds. Emphasize that there is no excuse in your mind for lying to a lover about another lover. Show that you have a strict code of sexual ethics, and you will be better trusted for it.

5. That you publicly show that you have genuine affection and respect for your lovers without being artificially gushy about it. Be prepared to be a public example of honorable, loving polyamorous behavior; these people will be watching you to see if you're really all you make your lifestyle out to be. Be prepared to be on your best behavior for the first year or so.

6. That by living successfully in this lifestyle, you are prepared to be the "Polyamory Answer Person" and talk to all the members of the group who will hesitantly wander over and ask questions about your lifestyle. When they do so, please remember point #1.

One of the first things that you can do is to have a talk with the leaders of the group and ask them how you can best get these messages across. How the leaders treat you will have a strong effect on how others treat you, especially since they may question the leaders about you before they feel comfortable asking you directly. Make sure that the leaders have their facts straight and are clear on your wish to make people comfortable with your family without your having to hide and sacrifice yourselves. A good leader will respond with appreciation to your willingness to work toward group harmony.

It may seem unfair and arbitrary to have to reassure people in this way, but sometimes we have to make hard choices between what is fair and what is effective. To be the first person from a particular minority to enter a group is to be their first—and often crucial—example of what that minority is like. You are, by default, the educator. It's best to keep this in mind, whatever message you choose to send.

You are also a messenger of the new era in relationships, where people are free to love in whatever way works for them. If we want this ideal to spread throughout society—and if you're reading this book, it's likely that you do—we will have to acknowledge that every one of us gets the job of being its ambassador. It's more than just our own personal ideas that we're bringing to a space, it's the dismantling of the current limiting status quo around sex and gender, which has been around for many hundreds of years and will be difficult to root out. When you walk into a spiritually oriented group, being a living symbol and avatar of change, you bring change with you like a virus. To be fully integrated into that group is to disrupt their worldview and alter it.

This is especially important when we remember that the Pagan worldview holds sexuality as sacred. Pagans frequently talk about how sacred it is, without really understanding what that means; there's a lot of mouthing of that line in *The Charge of the Goddess* about all acts of love and pleasure being her rituals, but what does that entail in the everyday? It's more than just "sex is good, it's not a nasty thing like the sex-negative religions say." It's more than knowing that you can use sexual energy for magical purposes. It's the concept that when we are surrendering to our sexual needs and desires, whatever they are, we are in one of the states of consciousness that is closest to our surrendering to Divine Will. That's why sex magic works, when it actually works: you're just one jump away.

Sexual energy, and the energy of sexual love that comes with it, is like an all-rushing tide that can sweep you away. The love goddesses are always intoxicating, no matter which one you're talking about. However, like all pure forms of divine energy, they have their particular blind spots. One of them is that they value that lived experience of surrender to the sweeping wave more than they value such down-to-earth things as rules and commitments. Aphrodite may have gotten married to Hephaestus, but she slept frequently with other gods and mortals, even when that infuriated him. To her, there was nothing unethical about it; it's foolish to think that one can so contain a love goddess.

Similarly, the African love goddess Oshun never tied herself to one husband, although she favored the fiery orisha Shango. Freyja gave herself to whomever she pleased, including taking gold or jewelry for her favors, and thought no less of herself. Ishtar chose a different consort each year, if she so desired. Krishna multiplied himself so as to be able to have sex with hundreds of women, and it was considered a blessing for him to touch one of them.

However, we are not gods and goddesses. We are mere mortals, and as such we have to deal with rules and boundaries and be considerate of others in a way that divine powers don't have to deal with. I see being polyamorous in a sacred way, similar to how Gaea manages the ecosystem. Everything has to be in balance, but that balance isn't stasis. It's constant readjustment of this factor and that factor. To have healthy and sacred polyamorous relationships is to treat your love life like an ecosystem, with all the respect that we as Pagans should have for the actual ecosystem. If too much attention is paid to sun, there will be a drought. If too much attention is paid to rain, there will be a flood. When something goes out of balance, you have to make the hard decision as to whether overcompensation in the other direction will even things out or make things worse, like the floodwaters eroding the dried-out soil. Watching the flora and fauna that appear and disappear can tell you a lot about how well the system is working, which means keeping a vigilant eye on small signs, the relationship equivalent of frogs and insects.

Just as it is a sacred work when you're planting trees and picking up trash, it is also sacred when you're dashing from one lover's weepy crisis to the other lover's moving day. It is a discipline of love, loyalty, and balance. Being polyamorous has taught me more about the real nature of romantic love, committed love, loyalty, and generosity than I ever could have learned in fifty years of being monogamous.

As I researched information and interviewed people for this book, in and out of the Pagan community, I did get a sense of how Pagan polyamory was different not only from secular polyamory but also from the spiritual approach of non-Pagans to this relationship style. Although I may be the first writer to widely disseminate a Pagan approach to it, I am hardly the first person to write or talk about "spiritual polyamory" in general. It seems, however, that most of the other people who are talking and writing about it are coming from a transcendent Eastern-religion approach, which contrasts strongly with the Pagan worldview.

It's not that there's anything wrong with a transcendent Eastern-religion worldview; it's just that writing from that perspective does not help the practitioners of an earth-centered, body-centered, immanent religion find a useful model. It seemed like all the non-Pagans that I spoke to about spiritual polyamory were coming at it from a perspective of nonattachment, as part of a larger discipline of nonattachment toward the entire world. Their approach to polyamory seemed to be working toward being less passionately attached to all of their lovers (and in some cases to everything in general), and that once they had achieved this, they would no longer feel any jealousy, or any of the inconvenient emotions that come up in complicated relationships. Many of them attributed their acceptance of polyamory directly to a practice of emotional nonattachment.

Although, as I said, nonattachment is a perfectly valid spiritual practice, it's not the way this is done within a Pagan cosmology. The love goddesses resent the idea that anyone would want to feel less passionate about anything. To us Pagans, polyamory is about having passionate attachments to more than one person, and learning how best to handle that without sacrificing one bit of the intensity. It's about learning to handle riding the wild horse, rather than exchanging it for a tamer one or deciding that these horses are just too much trouble. I worry, too, that those polyfolk who are doing the nonattachment path in an unskillful way may use it as an excuse to ignore or deny important emotional issues rather than dealing with them, and in the process either build up a secret fund of "unacceptable" feelings or empty their relationships of depth and intensity.

The Pagan worldview is one of fully embracing the world, rather than trying to escape it; of willingly embodying joy and pain and everything in between, and every nuance of love and sorrow as too sacred to forgo. We open our hearts willingly and accept that even the risk of pain is worth the lessons learned and the gifts given. To treat those gifts with anything less than our wholehearted passion is to dishonor and insult the Source from whence they flow.

Polyamorous Interfaith Wedding

This polyamorous interfaith wedding ceremony was sent to me just too late to make it into my book on handfastings, and it more appropriately belongs here anyway. It was created by a Michigan triad that consisted of one Pagan, one Jew, and one Christian. They wrote to me: "In a way, it was a good thing that this was a polyamorous relationship that couldn't be legally validated anyway. We'd all spent years in dyadic relationships with people of other faiths, and we'd all sat up late at night wondering about what kind of an interfaith wedding we could create that wouldn't make all the in-laws hate us. When it became clear that we were going to be asking them to not only accept that we were marrying a member of another faith, but two members of two other faiths, everything became much clearer and simpler. It was no longer a matter of how to make our relationship socially acceptable. There was no way to make it socially acceptable, not anymore. Those who cared and loved us for who we were would come. Those who couldn't bring themselves to come, well, they were that many fewer people we'd have to cater to. We could be assured that even if our wedding had an audience of ten people, they'd be ten people who were with us wholeheartedly."

The ceremony took place outdoors. There were three people acting as clergy. Since the triad was unable to find a Jewish rabbi or Christian minister willing to deal with them, and since the Pagan member did not belong to an organized Pagan group or tradition, they chose to have three close friends act as clergy. These friends were each chosen for their faith and knowledge in the religion of their choice and their loyalty to the triad's bond. They consisted of a Quaker lesbian currently in seminary, a Talmudic scholar, and a Radical Faery priest. They are designated as Clergy 1, 2, and 3, respectively.

First, the quarters were cast by four friends of the Pagan member of the triad. They elected not to use deity names, but simply called the elements of earth, water, fire, and air in their capacity as guardians of body, heart, spirit, and mind. The Pagan member of the triad walked the circle with a torch, representing their fierce passion, which was then planted in the middle of the field.

The Jewish member of the triad had suggested that they put together a ketubah, which is a formal, poetic contract stating their intentions for the marriage. Ketubahs are a Jewish custom, but these days some interfaith Christian-Jewish weddings are also creating their own. This ketubah was created by all three lovers and was read aloud by the mother of the Jewish partner.

"This ketubah witnesses before the God of Abraham, the Name of Christ, and all the holy gods and goddesses who smile upon us, and before the eyes of those who value our souls and our love, that the sacred covenant of marriage was entered into between _____, _____, and _____. Surrounded by loving community, we affirm our commitment to each other as lovers, spouses, and friends. Our lives are now forever intertwined. Love, loyalty, patience, and understanding will always be the foundation of our home together. We will celebrate all the passages of life together with joy, reverence, appreciation of our differences, and delight in our common affinities. Let this document be a pledge of our constant faith and our abiding devotion. We willingly enter into this covenant, sharing our hearts, bodies, minds, and spirits until the tides of time end us on this blessed Earth."

Clergy 1: Welcome, family and friends of these lovers who ask to be bound together here before your eyes. Your presence and solidarity blesses us all. We ask that you surround them in a circle of love as unconditional as God's love.

Clergy 2: Welcome, people of the community in which they will find safe harbor. Your presence and witnessing gives us hope for the future. We ask that you see their wedding today as a bridge between many traditions, which future generations may cross.

Clergy 3: Welcome, you who will go forth and speak about this day. Your presence affirms that we are all part of one world and that love can be the magnet that pulls a tribe together. We ask that you see their wedding today as a bridge between old bonds and new patterns, which will inspire everyone they meet.

Clergy 1: Divine Providence, we rejoice in your life in the midst of our lives. You are the light illuminating everyone; you show us the way and the life. You love us even when we are unfaithful. You sustain us with your Holy Spirit. We praise you for your presence with us and especially in the act of solemn covenant. Amen. I would like to take this moment to mention those who are close to these lovers but could not be here today. Our thoughts and blessings are with them as well, as we can only hope that theirs are with us.

Clergy 2: Blessed are you, O God, for giving life, sustaining us and bringing us to this joyous time. I would like to take this moment to mention that these blessed lovers have loved ones who are no longer here in body, but who are here in spirit. Let us remember them now in a moment of silence.

Clergy 3: Lady of Light and Darkness, in the dust of whose feet are the hosts of heaven, whose body encircles the universe; grant your blessing to these lovers who stand here before you to be joined as one. Lord of Darkness and Light, seed sower, Horned One, dancer in the heart; grant your blessing to these lovers who stand here before you to be joined as one. I would like to take this moment to mention the sacred ancestors, without whose life and toil we would not be here today. I believe that they would be proud of this moment.

Clergy 1: I shall betroth thee unto me forever. Yea, I shall betroth thee unto me in righteousness and in loving kindness and in compassion; and I shall betroth thee unto me in faithfulness. Do you, _____, come here today to be joined in marriage to _____ and _____, to have and to hold, to love and to cherish, in good times and bad, in sickness and in health, with one heart between you?

Christian member of the triad says, "I do."

Clergy 2: Blessed are you who come here in the name of God. Serve God with joy, come into God's presence with song. O most awesome, glorious, and blessed God, grant your blessings to these lovers. Do you, _____, come here today to be joined in marriage to _____ and _____, being faithful to them, protecting their hearts and defending their love, sharing happiness and sorrow, with one heart between you?

Jewish member of the triad says, "I do."

Clergy 3: Holy Lady in your form of the Bride, be with us today. Horned One in your season of love, be with us today. Do you, _____, come here today to be joined in marriage to _____ and _____, sharing the warmth of your body, the light of your mind, and the joy of your spirit, with one heart between you?

Pagan member of the triad says, "I do."

Clergy 1: May God bless you and keep you. May his countenance shine upon you and be gracious to you. We now pronounce you married!

Clergy 2: May God look upon you with favor and grant you peace. You were three; now you are one. Shalom!

Clergy 3: May the peace of all the gods be with you all the days of your life. Blessed be! You can now kiss. *(All three kiss each other.)*

The Christian member of the triad wanted to do a unity candle as part of the ceremony. They each chose a taper candle in their favorite colors and one large white pillar candle that they carved with their initials and symbols of their love. Carving the candle was a week-long project; it sat on the kitchen table next to a sharp knife, and they traded off working on it.

Clergy 1: In the wedding liturgy, candlelight symbolizes the commitment of love declared on the wedding day. Before you, you see four special candles. The three smaller candles symbolize the lives of these three lovers. Until today, all have let their light shine as individuals in their respective communities. Now they have come to publicly proclaim their love in the new union of marriage. They do not lose their individuality. Yet, in marriage, they are united in so close a bond that they become one. Now they will light the large center candle from the smaller candles, to symbolize this new reality. In this way they are saying that henceforth their light must shine together for each other, for their families, and for the community.

Each member of the triad lit their candle, saying, "This is the light of my soul," and then all three lit the large candle, saying in unison, "You are the lights of my life." Then a glass of wine was brought out by a friend.

Clergy 2: This cup of wine has many meanings. The first is that wine is a symbol of the sweetness we wish for your life. There will be times when you drink from other cups, from bitter ones; but life offers opportunity to savor the sweetness. The awareness of the possibility of a life filled with true meaning is what we toast: the good that is life. The second is that wine is a symbol of sharing. You have shared many years together, and out of this time has grown the love which brought you to this day. As you continue to share in each other's life, you will, as a symbol of this enduring cooperation, share this cup of wine. Blessed are you, O God, creator of the fruit of the vine. *(All three drink from the glass.)* There are many different explanations for the breaking of the glass. Originally, it was said that it was broken because it could never be used again for anything quite so sacred. Today, the fragility of the glass suggests the frailty of human relationships. The glass is broken to protect this marriage with the implied prayer: May your bond of love be as difficult to break as it would be to put together the pieces of this glass. *(The glass is stepped on, and several prompted friends call out, "Mazel tov!")*

Clergy 3: This broom isn't fancy; it's the broom that you use to sweep your house every day. As such, it represents the ordinary, niggling tasks that you will have to share with each other. Take hands and jump over it, showing that you will leap these small problems together, hand in hand, as a team. *(All three take hands and jump the broom. Everyone applauds, and the rite is over.)*

Uranus

The Tribe and the Community

"We believe that polyamory is a very important new relationship option whose time seems to have arrived. Where once we thought that every family should consist of a monogamous man and woman with their 2.5 kids, we now know that a family is any small group of bonded people who claim that connection with each other. Most families no longer fit the conventional description. The much-lamented 'breakdown of the American family' and the need to reclaim 'traditional family values' are manifestations of the twentieth century's transition from village life with extended families to the modern 'nuclear family' units, which these days often reduce down to a single mother trying to raise and support children she hardly interacts with.

"A century ago, the typical American family consisted of three generations or more living together in the same house, along with lateral relatives such as uncles and aunts, and possibly an unrelated live-in servant such as a housekeeper. The 'traditional American family,' in fact, looked more like *The Addams Family*. But with each generation of the last century we have become more isolated and alienated. Ever-increasing numbers of American children are growing up with hardly any parental interactions and no adult role models for parenting or other relationships. Their interactions with other children occur in hostile environments, such as schools and the street, where they are subject to ever-rising levels of teasing, harassment, bullying, and violence. They retreat to the world of television, video games, and the Internet, none of which provide real-life interaction with actual flesh-and-blood human beings.

"But deep within each of us is our genetic ancestral memory of the tribe, the clan, the extended family. Such a rich network of relationships nurtured our ancestors from the dawn of humanity, and it was within that context that we became fully human. We require and crave such connections in our deepest heart of hearts, and we seek them in clubs, gangs, fraternities, cliques, parties, pubs, communes, churches, covens, nests, and circles of close friends.

"For an increasing number of us, we are learning how to create such complex and deep bonding relationships through extended networks of multiple lovers and expanded families. Polyamory is both a new paradigm for relationships and a vision for healing the pathological alienation of individuals in modern society. We now know that the biodiversity we value in nature, as biologist Bruce Bagemihl points out, is valuable in sexual and bonding behavior as well. And although Dr. Bagemihl is talking about animals, we are also animals, and this applies equally to us. Polyamory is not 'the answer.' Diversity and choice are the answers, and polyamory is one of the strands in the decentralized network of diversity and choice in human bonding, intimacy, and family."

—THE ZELL-RAVENHEARTS, CALIFORNIA

In astrology, the planet Uranus is the forethinker, the harbinger of change—sometimes chaotic change that merely interferes, sometimes the stroke of genius that will change the world. It is also associated with all society, all people—tribe and clan and nation and world and universality. Uranus shines light on how we deal with each other in large groups and as a species intertwined in this web of life. It is the first of the transpersonal planets, the energies that work with the big picture rather than the small personal conflict. It is under the rule of Uranus that we learn about the impact that our personal relationships have on our larger community.

So is polyamory about the search for a tribe or is it just a personal ideal? The opinions on my survey were mixed; for some, polyamory never touched their political or spiritual life. For others, it was integrally entwined, a part of their spiritual value system.

Galadriel from Philadelphia writes that "my circle is my tribe. Some of us are poly and some of us are not. Some of us have been intimately connected at some point, and others have not . . . but I can see how it could strengthen bonds and community." Jen from Boston feels that the "poly as tribe" idea is overstating the case: "I think it's more of a way to create family. I think of 'tribe' as being a larger scale. I think of the whole Pagan community as a tribe; I think of the Jewish people as a tribe. I have seen poly clumps of people (folks with their lovers and their lovers' lovers) celebrating holidays together, living together, raising children together. I think that's more of a family thing, an extended family."

Colleen in Maryland warned, "I don't think that any Pagan tribe or community should ever require anyone to be poly, or be monogamous, or be whatever. It should be about acceptance of variety and diversity. We need to keep that in mind."

When I interviewed people in the Pagan demographic who were strongly against polyamory, their responses fell into three generalized categories. The first category contained people who simply felt that it wasn't "decent" or that it was "wrong," but their reasons were vague and tended to be strongly subjective. With a little pressure, nearly all of them revealed that they just weren't ready to question the social ideal of monogamy, even when that ideal was taken from the Judeo-Christian upbringings that they had abandoned.

In my mind, this is sloppy thinking. The individual who takes their rules of behavior directly from biblical sources has at least the argument "It's right because it's in the Bible," even if that argument makes no sense to anyone who does not share that faith and belief. The individual who has broken away from the faith that gave them their values, but never questions them, doesn't even have that excuse. To me, as a thinking modern Pagan, there's no difference between directly following the rules of the Bible and following the rules given to you by your parents or teachers who were following the rules of the Bible. If anything, it's worse; it shows a lack of willingness to examine your own standards and their validity.

Other reasons why polyamory was "wrong" came from people who tended to make the generalization "wrong for me, wrong for everyone"; they were unable or unwilling to step outside of their own feelings far enough to see how a different person might have other preferences. It's easy—and lazy—to simply imagine how you'd feel doing a particular practice, decide that you wouldn't like it and that it would be unpleasant for you, and conclude that it oughtn't be allowed. Some of this particular subset had actually dabbled with polyamory, had an unsuccessful experience, and were now convinced that it "couldn't work" and that long-term polyamorous families were probably ready to break up any time now. This is reminiscent of those embittered people who decide that marriage is an unworkable institution just because they got a divorce.

Some were worried about the effect of polyamory on children growing up in polyamorous families, although even if that was their only complaint, I had difficulty getting them to agree that it would be ethical for adults with no children. Some seemed to feel that the problem was that children might see polyamory as a legitimate option and take it as adults—although again, if that was their only complaint, it was rather a circular argument. Some were honestly worried about children being "confused" over who their parents actually were, which is a legitimate issue that led me to take a great deal of care with the moon chapter in this book. In general, I encouraged them to talk to children of polyamorous parents and get their fears alleviated.

Some people complained about Pagans who are worried about the image of their religion getting too "radical" or "strange" in the eyes of outsiders. In general, the feeling among polyamorous Pagans was, as Alex from Massachusetts said, "If people are determined to dislike Pagans, they'll find a reason. So to me it's irrelevant what anyone thinks."

One triad complained that "there is a growing minority in the Pagan demographic who wish to dumb down Paganism in order to make it more acceptable to the conservative elements of the general populace. Aside from polyamory, we have heard criticism of skyclad worship and anything involving blood, to name a few. For ourselves, we feel that this is beyond ridiculous, and is both insulting and potentially devastating. We believe that many of the people supposedly trying to make Paganism more palatable to the masses are in fact not completely comfortable with it themselves."

Galadriel in Philadelphia says, "I think the demographic concerned with this are the Pagans who are trying to make Paganism mainstream. There are benefits to being mainstream and accepted by the wider community, but on the other hand, if we get too mainstream and PC, we lose something in the process. I think my aversion to this is the same as my aversion to magic "Wicca 101" books geared to the masses and especially to teens. I feel in some way that we are diluting our traditions so that modern-day America may accept us better. I'm not sure this is necessarily the best thing for the Pagan community to do. The words 'fluffy bunny,' 'Sunday Pagans,' and 'dabblers' come to mind."

Colleen and other Pagans stressed the importance of diversity as a Pagan value: "Pagans are a diverse group. We are inclusive, not exclusive, and we should remain that way. If we change to fit politically or socially current standards, are we still Pagan? And what then have we gained if we lose our sense of self? If all is sacred, does that actually mean 'all' or only 'nearly all,' or 'some,' or 'those who practice this gender identity or that type of marriage'?"

PolyPagan of the Waterkin from New Zealand is more blunt: "What do I think of those people in the community? Get a life! Get more and better sex! Drop your control mode! Seriously—polyamory is the path of the future. Get used to it!" He also stresses that "it's very, very important for poly people to educate others on what it's really about. The survival of humanity, peace in the world, and the future of our children depends on it."

Ruth in Massachusetts snarls, "The people who say that polyamory is bad for the community? Bite me! I am getting really sick of the 'all whatevers do this because some whatevers do this.' All Christians aren't evil because your mom was a Christian and she beat you, all Satanists aren't evil because you don't understand them, and all Pagans aren't poly because I am. I'm sick of that, okay? Sick of it. Just because I am poly doesn't mean that I will force you to be. It's kind of like my sexual preference, okay?"

Most polyfolk were clear that polyamory wasn't for everyone and agreed that most people were monogamous and shouldn't be criticized for that personal limitation. Some even claimed that polyamory shouldn't be practiced by people who couldn't get "ordinary" monogamy right. Generally, though, the consensus was that polyfolk should stick to dating other polyfolk and not pressure monogamous people to try out their preference.

A small but vocal minority of polyfolk were more radical in their opinions, proclaiming adamantly that anyone could be poly if they were only to try. PolyPagan of the Waterkin from New Zealand insists, "Polyamory is the natural way for human beings to relate. The only difficulty is finding what we're really about, relearning what's been wrenched out of us or not properly taught and modeled for us, and dealing with stupid judgmental attitudes and responses from the stupefied society in which we live. If those people had no ability to affect us in damaging ways, we'd have no problems at all."

This attitude, while provocative and interesting to consider, has created some enemies of polyamory in the Pagan community. Brenna from Wisconsin admits that she cringes "when I hear people say things like, 'everyone is really polyamorous, they just don't know it.' It's the kind of missionary overcompensation that people do when they've just discovered something really fulfilling, and in their overenthusiasm they think that because it's right for them, it would probably be right for everyone. Some people are just born evangelists, and they can't seem to get it into their heads that whatever their current love is, is not going to be everyone's love. You just have to patiently keep repeating to them the very Pagan mantra of 'your way is not my way, but it's okay. Everyone has a different path.' If they hear it enough times, maybe they'll get it. In the meantime, you can smile and nod and completely ignore their zeal."

Tim from New Jersey complains that "the poly evangelists hurt our chances of ever getting polyamory accepted as a legitimate lifestyle within the Pagan community because they make monogamous people feel disrespected for their choices. On the other hand, some monogamous people feel that we make Paganism in general impossible to get accepted by non-Pagans, just by existing, so I suppose there are people on both sides who need to get smacked with a clue-by-four."

Jen from Boston pleads, "I would like you to give a nod to monogamy in this book, so that you can acknowledge it as a valid relationship structure too." It's actually an area of contention among poly people: whether or not some people are just "naturally" polyamorous while others are "naturally" monogamous, or whether anyone can stretch to fit either mold at will. For myself, I am quite sure that I am incapable of being happy in a monogamous relationship, and I have never managed one successfully in my entire life. That would tend to make me fall into the "naturally nonmonogamous" category. For a while, I tended to assume that other people divided up just as strongly to one side or the other and that it was simply a matter of built-in personality as to which side one fell on.

However, as time went on, I met and spoke to people who went happily back and forth between monogamous and polyamorous relationships, adjusting to the wishes of their partner. Karen from New England talks about this situation: "I never thought in a million years that I would be a poly person. It just never caught my attention. Now I can't imagine having stayed monogamous. However, depending on my primary partner, I could probably very easily be poly or not poly. I do what works with the people that I am with. If things should change between my husband and myself—if we no longer get along and split, or he should die—I may not choose to stay polyamorous. The next person will help determine that. However, I hope my husband and I have a long life together. He has shown me that loving more than one person does not mean you love the other less. I'm thankful for that lesson."

Tim from New Jersey agrees: "I could probably adapt to being monogamous, if my lover really wanted it and we were compatible enough to get at least a fair amount of my needs met. No, one lover can't meet all my needs, but then I don't think I could ever get enough lovers to meet all my needs! Right now I have one primary, who is poly, and I'm fine with that. I have two women that I see casually—friends with whom I cuddle and have sex—but they aren't serious. The problem would be if I had a serious second lover, and then I got told by my primary that we were going to be monogamous. I couldn't do that; choosing would be too painful. But if I had no one serious, I think I could adapt."

There are more reasons for people to dislike polyamory, however, than just a conservative non-Pagan upbringing and worries about public relations. On one email list of mixed Pagans and Heathens, a verbal scuffle ensued between the polyamorous members and those who felt that it was outright wrong but weren't able to rationally discuss what was specifically wrong. All the participants on that side of the line were heterosexual women; the polyfolk were mixed male and female. When the dust settled and a whole lot of gentle and courteous probing had gone on, the reality of the situation came out. For every one of the women in question, polyamory raised deep fears of abandonment. They were monogamous and preferred things that way, yet they all believed on some level that their male husbands and boyfriends would, if given the chance, prefer to be polyamorous and would attempt to pressure them into it. If polyamory was universally condemned in their religious communities— as it was in mainstream religious communities—they would be able to respond negatively with the boost of the high moral ground. On the other hand, with polyamory on display as an acceptable alternative, they felt that they would be under constant pressure from their male lovers to "convert."

This attitude, which I've actually found to be disturbingly widespread, springs from the idea that women naturally prefer monogamy while men are horndogs who would, given a chance, screw anything in sight. In Morning Glory Zell-Ravenheart's article *A Bouquet of Lovers* (see appendix III), she caustically quotes the old rhyme, "Hogamus higamus, men are polygamous; higamus hogamus, women monogamous." It also has very old roots in the sexist practices of polygamy in traditional cultures, where men are allowed to have several partners while women must remain sexually faithful.

In reality, men have as many issues with polyamory in practice as women do. They get jealous, they feel left out, they press for monogamy. I know as many poly women who are monogamous for the sake of their male partners as I do poly men who refrain out of love for their girlfriends and wives. Men can also eventually find that they would rather have depth of emotion than simply a large number of shallow encounters, although it may take them longer due to factors such as hormone levels and social stereotyping.

There's also the fact that no social group is obligated to pass rules so as to allow people to shirk doing work on their relationship. It's the same reason that many married women in older days supported laws against adultery and still support laws against prostitution today—*let the state force my husband to be faithful, because I can't seem to do it. Let society tell my boyfriend that he should be sexually exclusive, because he won't listen to me.* It seems painfully obvious to me that if he won't listen to you and take your feelings into account, perhaps he's not worth your time. Ideally, the reason why spouses should hold to a mutually-agreed-upon pact around their appropriate level of chosen sexual exclusivity is to prevent them from hurting each other. If the idea of hurting you is not enough for your spouse, then it's unlikely that social and religious guilt will stop him. Certainly it hasn't done a very good job of it so far; something like 60 percent of monogamous marriages experience cheating at least once in their duration.

The problem is that you as the poly person are not going to be able to assuage these fears. Perhaps, with time and patience, you can convince the reluctant people in the Pagan community that it's not technically harmful (even if it seems to them that it ought to be, somehow, even though they can't put their finger on it), that it can work (even if not for them), that it won't alienate every non-Pagan (and the ones that it does would have rejected us for something else anyway), that we are not going to disrespect their commitment bonds, and that children are not harmed by being raised in poly families. There is absolutely no way that you can convince a stranger that their partner will not pressure them to be polyamorous once they've seen you successfully demonstrate it. It might happen, it might not, but if they're scared of it, there's no way to alleviate that fear . . . and if they're speaking from that fear, they may be pretty hostile.

The only thing to do is to be patient with them, be as compassionate as you can force yourself to be, and to trust in the long, slow change of social mores. Eventually, if all goes well, the rigid rules around relationships will soften, and more people will be interested in learning how to be more communicative and have better intimacy with each other. One would hope, anyway. In such a climate, there would hopefully be fewer problems with this level of distrust in couples.

You—and your out-of-the-closet, aboveboard, healthy, public, polyamorous family—are part of that long-term solution. Don't forget that fact in the face of irrational anger and hostility. You are important to the greater Pagan community because you help it stretch and grow by example. Sometimes stretching and growing hurts. Ask any out member of the GLBT community—and then ask them why they're out of the closet. You may have to be in the closet about poly for your job, or even for your aging grandmother, but don't let your Pagan religious community off so easily. They—we— ought to know better. Give them a chance to learn.

Ritual for Creating a Pagan Tribe

Are you looking for a tribe? This ritual is a way of asking the Powers That Be to send you the right people. The catch is that there must be at least three of you to start with, or possibly two who are not romantically involved. If a single person or a couple in relationship does this ritual, you may be drawn to an already existing tribe (which may be fine with you!), but you will not have disparate people drawn to you to form your own group. So this ritual is for a small clan looking to create a larger tribe. If there are already at least three of you— three being a magic number—then it's fine if you're all romantically involved.

Start out by creating a shrine to this tribe that you desire. Set up a specific place that won't be disturbed, even if only a small shelf.

Discuss between you the sort of qualities that you are looking for in this future tribe, and lay cloth in colors that symbolize those qualities. (Examples: brown for hard work, green for ecology consciousness, black for commitment, gold for financial stability, blue for sanity, red for passion, pink for romance, yellow for cheerfulness, and so forth.) As you lay them down, speak those qualities aloud.

Next, each of you should look for things that symbolize other qualities that you want for this tribe, and lay them on the altar. Examples that we've seen in the past:

- A broom and dustpan for willingness to do boring chores.

- A metal chain to symbolize commitment and the willingness to hang together.

- A small crown for honor and noble behavior.

- Bandages, for mutual efforts to heal each other.

- Ceremonial weapons, for the willingness to defend each other. These should be placed near the edge of the shrine, pointed outwards and not inwards.

- Symbols of various gender and sexual preferences.

- Sex toys for open-mindedness about sexuality.

- A mirror, that the tribe might be a vehicle for self-knowledge.

- Religious objects, that there might be a common spiritual bond.

- Symbols of shared political values—pamphlets, books, or more direct symbols such as a green branch for ecology, a dove for peace, a female figure for feminism, a set of scales filled with coins for belief in fair capitalism, or whatever it is that you are looking for.

- Bread or a bowl of some other food, that all might nourish each other.

- A fishnet, that the tribe might be a safety net to catch each other.

- The figure of an open hand, for sharing.

- Symbols of particular skills or crafts, such as knitting needles, nails for carpentry, a trowel for gardening, a wrench for mechanical skills, etc.

- Salt, for common sense.

- Small toy cars, if it's important that people have their own transportation.

- Open mouths, for communication.

- Money. It seems important that actual money be put on the shrine, even if only a few coins. If there will hopefully be shared finances, it is important that the money be left openly on the shrine, rather than stuck in a box or envelope. If some-one walks through your house and swipes it, consider it an offering to the Powers That Be and replace it good-humoredly, which will encourage mutual generosity.

Make sure that each item is approved by all of you. If it makes even one person feel distinctly uncomfortable, the issue should be discussed before it goes on. This is a group effort, not a chance for one person to create their own fantasy. Every item on the altar should be wholeheartedly approved of by everyone doing this ritual or it could sabotage the direction of the energy.

Stand before the shrine. Hold hands, if it is appropriate to your personal style of affection. If not, at least stand together as a committed group. Now take one final item that has heretofore been kept off the shrine: a magnet, the bigger the better. Pass it from hand to hand among each other as you say the following:

> Spirits of the elements,
>
> Air and water, fire and earth,
>
> Spirits of the spaces between,
>
> The unknown and the mystery,
>
> Gods who listen, goddesses hear us!
>
> Our minds are magnets that draw our tribe to us.
>
> Our hearts are mage-nets that gather them together.
>
> Our souls are shining stars that lead them home.
>
> Our bodies are standing stones that mark the end of the road.
>
> We call you, tribe that will be named _____, and _____,
>
> and _____, (insert appropriate names and/or qualities)
>
> By the light of these our hopes,
>
> By the building of our hands,
>
> By the yearning of our dreams,
>
> By the voices of our combined will.
>
> We call you home to us!
>
> May all the gods lead you to our door
>
> And may you find it welcome.

The magnet is placed on the altar, and each person repeats, "Welcome." Now go away and wait for the spell to work. These things take time, perhaps even months or years; your job is to recognize when someone is sent and when they're just passing through. Bringing them before the altar, without telling them its purpose, and seeing their instinctive reaction may help you to decide.

Neptune

Ideals and Illusions

Astrologically, Neptune is the planet of both higher spiritual mysticism and delusion, holy altered state and drugged-out daze. With Neptune, it's hard to know what's real and what's just a projection of your own needs. This is also a problem with polyamory, and the myths aren't just the ones covered in the first chapter, which are the misconceptions of outsiders. Those of us who practice polyamory sometimes slip into idealistic dreams that sometimes turn out to be false later.

One such myth is the starry-eyed view that just starting to practice polyamory will automatically make you into an unselfish person in record time. Although polyamory can be a wonderful vehicle for spiritual growth and development, it's never a quick and easy solution, but rather a long and difficult path with many final rewards. To integrate polyamory into one's spiritual path, a commitment must be made to acknowledging one's illusions and trying one's best to get rid of them. Being poly won't make you less jealous, for example, unless you are deliberately using poly specifically as a tool to stretch and hone yourself. That sort of thing takes time and hurts a lot. It's difficult, especially the part about giving up illusions. We like our illusions, and it takes a lot of effort for us to uncurl our clenched fists and let go of them. This is especially true when some of those illusions have been down in print for decades, and they're what people run into when they look for cultural icons of polyamory.

The single book that seems to have affected the growth of poly-amory the most can likely be Robert Heinlein's *Stranger in a Strange Land*. For those who haven't read it, the rather dubious plot centers around a human raised by Martians and returned to Earth as an adult; since his upbringing is entirely devoid of human social con-cepts, he finds himself constantly confused by and at war with Earth culture. Eventually, he starts his own polyamorous cult, where every-one develops mysterious psychic powers. (One of my lovers con-fessed to me that when he read about the cult, it wasn't the polyamory that caught his eye, it was all that stuff about learning telekinesis!) However clumsily, the book introduced the concept of accepted, widespread polyamory into the demographic of readers of fantasy and science fiction, and it spread from there in the comparatively permissive climate of the 1960s.

I am entirely unsure about whether Heinlein actually practiced any form of polyamory, and as he's dead, we can't ask him. However, his vision of this form of loving was woefully idealized; no one is ever jealous or insecure, everyone seems to sleep with everyone else without any negotiation or second thoughts, and of course there's never any venereal disease (perhaps due to all those enhanced psy-chic powers). Since the book did not postulate a future culture where polyamory is so accepted that everyone's learned how to deal with it, but with a "modern" bunch of people who move in with a Martian and are suddenly old hands at the practice, it did have unfortunate side effects. An embarrassing number of people rushed straight for polyamory—and in some cases, pure promiscuous nonmonogamy—and expected it to end up like Heinlein's fictional vision. Brenna in Wisconsin says, "We were terribly disappointed when we and our lovers didn't suddenly lose all feelings of wanting to keep someone to ourselves, and there was a lot of drama and people calling each other unenlightened. If only that book had shown us one episode of someone having a problem like that and working it out!"

Forty years later, the *Stranger* ideal still refuses to die. The Church of All Worlds was founded largely on the strength of that book, although it later slid into being a Neopagan-style church with only a few of its original Heinleinian flourishes. Especially among demographics such as science fiction fans (who call themselves "fen" and have a lavish calendar of their own conventions), polyamory is seen as "the wave of the future," a new technology of relationships that supersedes old and outdated ways of loving. Of the SF conventions that I've been to (which have a significant overlap with the Pagan demographic), more than half have had panels on polyamory, and I've never seen the rooms less than completely filled, often to the point of standing-room only and people spilling out into the halls.

As long as we're discussing mystical utopias, this is probably a good place to bring up the Pagan festival and the notorious concept of "festival polyamory." In general, festivals tend to be a place where being out about poly isn't terribly dangerous. Jen in Boston recounts that "saying 'This is my primary/secondary' is a pretty well-received mode of introduction at festivals." Some couples are monogamous for most of the year, but allow each other some limited nonmonogamy at festivals, feeling that the "sacred space" makes the place safe for such experimenting. This has been referred to as "festival polyamory." That term has also been used more disparagingly to describe people who come to festivals without their monogamous significant other, claim to be polyamorous for the duration of the festival in order to get laid, and then go back to monogamy and their unwitting lover on Monday.

Festivals also tend to be the place where many people are first introduced to the concept of polyamory, as they run into and discuss with other Pagans from different traditions. Some people, like Brenna, discovered real polyamory in this setting. Pagan festivals often feel like a "time out of time and space out of space," as Pagans say about ritual circles. Sometimes they are clothing optional; sometimes there is a great deal of sexual energy from having so many sex-positive people together in one safe place. We as Pagans honor and revere sexuality as a sacred force, so it's not surprising that our festivals are more sexually free than, say, a Baptist convention. This can be a wonderful thing for some people and a difficult thing for others.

On the other hand, there's also a phenomenon that a friend refers to as "polycrackhead syndrome," which rears its head all too frequently at Pagan festivals. Someone will discover the concept of polyamory without yet understanding all the negotiating and compromises that are required to do it ethically. They are absolutely intoxicated with the idea, especially if they only see it as a way to get as much nookie as possible without getting in trouble. They inform their heretofore monogamous partner, who is horrified. Either a fight breaks out between the two of them or the other partner avoids talking about it . . . which their would-be-poly partner takes as permission and hops into the sack with the first nonmonogamous warm body who's willing and available. Of course, this creates another explosion, and the couple leave the gathering barely talking. Not infrequently, the "wronged" partner blames it on the presence of all those "loose" and "slutty" polyamorous Pagans who corrupted their partner with bad ideas.

As a way to head this off at the pass, I created the "Pagan Festival Polyamory Etiquette" flyer, found in appendix V. Much of the trouble of polycrackhead syndrome can be laid at the doorstep of two problems: lack of information and lack of communication. The first one can be remedied. The second one is harder, because there's no way that we as a community can force a couple to communicate with each other over anything. However, we can encourage people to communicate better with strangers that they meet at gatherings, which can perhaps circumvent some of the many ways that it's possible to screw up sexually at gatherings.

Sometimes, the many Pagan traditions that collect at festivals and gatherings can create a culture clash, and polyamory is often one of the hot-button topics in such explosions. "At Pagan festivals twenty years ago, it was gay issues," says Judie, "and you had heterosexuals freaking out at naked queers hugging each other in public. There were a lot of discussion groups, some of which degenerated into explosions and people storming out. Now polyamory is in the same hot seat in the Pagan community. I think that this can be remedied by more workshops on polyamory and how it fits into Pagan values—held not just for polyfolk, but for curious others."

Not all Pagan traditions hold the same values, and even some specific groups within a single tradition may have very different value systems as well. Some covens and groups will not allow GLBT members, as they work with extremely gender-polarized and heterosexual deities and feel that nonheterosexual members will foul up the magical polarity. There's also the fact, as one respondent commented in a prior chapter, that Neopaganism is still finding its feet with regard to an actual system of ethics and values. As it currently stands, it's vague enough that many Pagans don't bother to do anything except transplant their former (usually Judeo-Christian) value system without questioning it. This may be especially true if their relationship to Paganism, to date, has been mostly about magic and the occasional ritual, rather than any study of theology. Coming face to face with other traditions, not to mention the plethora of solitaries and all their religious diversity, can cause a bit of a brain explosion. It might be a good idea for larger festivals and gatherings to routinely hold introductory workshops and panels on how to cope with people whose beliefs don't exactly match your own, even if you are all technically part of the same religious community.

The "time out of time and space out of space" aspect of festivals may even aid this kind of ecumenicalism. There's something about "sacred space" that makes people feel that out-of-the-ordinary things are to be expected, and this makes them a little more psychologically flexible, or at least a little more willing to suspend their disbelief, while standing in the liminal space that Pagan festivals create. It makes them a good place to introduce new ideas, not for the sake of proselytizing—as one of the few core Pagan values that seems to cross traditional boundaries is a firm belief that proselytizing is rude and disrespectful—but to widen people's ideas of what is acceptable to at least some Pagan groups and traditions and how that fits into a Pagan worldview. This will only work, however, if festival staff are prepared enough to take advantage of their useful liminal space and its effects.

One thing that I heard over and over during interviews was people's certainty that their poly lovers were often contacts from past lives. This is markedly different from the more mainstream polyamorous community and made an interesting metaphysical argument for non-monogamy. Moira Wolf in Arizona says that "Nite and I feel that we've known each other in prior lives . . . and one of these days, I'm going to do some past-life regression to check that theory. But if we accept that we've lived before, then we must accept that we've loved before and that they [our lovers] might be reincarnated too. And since reincarnation doesn't run exactly linear—people die at different rates—your past loves might be here in this incarnation at different ages, if you find each other at all. What's to prevent more than one past love from being alive at the same time now? What's to prevent you from finding a new love in this lifetime? Should you forget a past love for a present love? Where does it say that you can only love one person at a time?"

Giovanni, Rachel, and JT are a V triad living in Florida who feel that they were married to each other before, more than once. Rachel explains: "Two hundred years ago, my parents arranged a marriage for me to an older man who is now my girlfriend JT in this lifetime. I slowly came to love him over time, but he was killed in a war while I was still young. I was surprised at how heartbroken I was . . . I clearly recall weeping at his grave, telling him that I wasn't yet done being his wife. At the same time, though, I'd been acquainted with a young man during that marriage, and I was half in love with him— might have been more so if the time and place hadn't deemed the very idea unfaithful. He courted and won me after my husband's death, and I lived out most of the rest of my life with him. In this life, their places are reversed . . . Giovanni met and married me first, and I recognized him as my second husband from that particular life- time. Except then JT came back into my life—this handsome, gallant butch dyke who is still so much a warrior—and I remembered what I'd said at his grave, all those years ago. And I had to make a decision, so I chose both! And never looked back."

Her partner JT has also been affected by past-life memories. "Gio and I didn't know each other in that lifetime except as passing acquaintances, so we don't have that bond of memory. But we both remember her! Sometimes I'll remember something about her from that lifetime, and I'll say, 'Rachel likes this,' and Gio will say, 'Yeah, I know she likes that,' and then Rachel will look confused because she's never done whatever we're talking about, and then we'll both realize that we're remembering what she liked two hundred years ago, and we'll sort of grin at each other and laugh sheepishly."

Dreamtime Tapestry Handfasting Ceremony

This ritual was created by a four-person polyamorous group who wanted a wedding ceremony that was completely different from any- thing that had been seen before. Instead of being the usual wedding- party-and-audience sort of ritual, it was designed to be completely participatory for everyone present. They set up a giant tapestry frame consisting of a five-foot-diameter circle of wood attached to two tall poles. The circle was detachable, so that it could eventually be hung on the wall of their home. It could be turned sideways on its attachments so that it was horizontal, or it could be made vertical.

They acquired wool in a variety of different colors, grown on the sheep farm of a friend and handspun and hand-dyed by local Pagan fiber artists. Everyone present was encouraged to bring a small charm or doodad of some kind—the invitation said "smaller than the palm of your hand"—with some way of attaching it. The charms symbolized good wishes that the attendees wanted for the marrying quadruple. Some of the charms included tiny mojo bags filled with herbs, salt, and powders; polished stones set with ring findings; metal jewelry pendants; tiny stained glass suncatchers; a bent silver spoon; tiny wreaths and brooms of dried flowers; a tiny jar of honey; old Yule ornaments; small dolls and toy people and animals; strings of beads; and packets of astrological soap.

They themselves each brought one of the following to the hand-fasting: a large colored scarf, a piece of polished stone shaped like a heart and hung with a ring, a slice of wood sawed from a tree limb with a bind-rune of their name and/or initials woodburned into it, and one unique charm of their own. As there were four of them, and they were each drawn to one particular element more than any other, the four scarves were in elemental colors. The stone hearts were made of minerals that symbolized their own personal qualities, although for those who want to reproduce this ritual, it could be any favorite stone. Make sure that they are all roughly equal in size. For the original ritual, the four lovers chose rose quartz, hematite, labradorite, and amethyst.

The night before, all their friends and family gathered together—no sex-segregated bachelor parties here—and wrapped yarn around and across the circular tapestry frame. Each turn was wrapped from side to side, crossing the middle like the spokes of a wheel or the outward-spreading strands of a spider's web. The strands were secured in the middle with a piece of colored yarn. The next day, the frame was hung up, filled in with the "warp," but otherwise empty.

The quarters were each called by one member of the "quad," as they called themselves, as follows:

East: *Love rises with the sun,*

Borne on winds of change,

Like a kiss gently brushing the forehead

Delicate as the touch of dragonflies

Mating on the cool spring breezes.

May we never forget that first moment of grace!

South: *Love blazes with the midday heat,*

Borne on fiery wings,

Like a kiss exploding on the lips

Passionate as a volcano's blast

Lighting up the summer sky.

May we never lose our glorious desire!

West: *Love caresses us like the falling twilight,*

Borne like a leaf on a river.

Like a kiss trickling over the curve of your heart

Loving as the ocean's tide

Dances with the shore in autumn.

May we never lose the flow of affection!

North: *Love warms our darkest nights,*

Born of the earth beneath our feet

Like a kiss offered to the deepest caves

Between thighs spread like mountain ranges

Under soft blankets of winter snow.

May we never break the bedrock of our commitment!

As each member of the quad invoked the element of their choice, they tied their scarf to the edge of the frame at the four compass points. They then stood together, before the company, and took out their ribbons. These are their quoted statements, but those who wish to use this ritual should choose their own colors and create their own. After describing their ribbons and their wishes, they each wove them between the "warp" threads, leaving the ends close enough to tie together.

Lover 1: This is the dream I have for our family: green as new spring leaves, always flexible like a young shoot, able to adapt to the coming year's weather, to bend and not to break.

Lover 2: This is the dream I have for our family: blue as a calm sky, serene and without a cloud, the meaning of peace and security, a safe place to come home to from the chaos of the outside world.

Lover 3: This is the dream I have for our family: the dark red of blood, sharing our fluids between us in this time of danger, creating bonds of shared blood to replace that of the blood kin that reject us, a clan tied together in good times and bad.

Lover 4: This is the dream I have for our family: the gold of inspiration, lighting up our days, remembering to be playful and take joy in life, giving us just enough closeness for comfort and just enough space for freedom.

At this point, each one brought out their charm and spoke about what they had brought. Again, people utilizing this ritual will want to pick their own; these are included for inspiration. As they speak about their ornaments, they tie them to the warp of the tapestry, near the center.

Lover 1: I bring to my loves a compass, that we might always know where we are going together. Because this much love would be wasted if we didn't use it to take us all somewhere better than we are now.

Lover 2: I bring to my loves this gift of my grandmother's old earrings, which she left to me. They hold the energy of a fifty-year solid and loving relationship between her and my grandfather, which was ended only by death, and I am sure that they are both together again today. They also symbolize heritage and tradition, which we are beginning here.

Lover 3: I bring to my loves this little screwdriver, because fixing things between people is something that I'm good at, and it's something that I value in this relationship. I want us to always be able to fix any problems that arise between us.

Lover 4: I bring to my loves cookies that I made yesterday and coated with shellac. They symbolize nourishment and sweetness, something that I hope we always have between us. I also bring some that have not been preserved for posterity, so we can share them with each other and with everyone here. (The lovers fed each other cookies, and then passed around the plate to everyone present. Then they brought out their stone hearts.)

Lover 1: My heart is yours. Like rose quartz, it is full of love.

Lover 2: My heart is yours. Like hematite, it is strong and grounding.

Lover 3: My heart is yours. Like labradorite, it sparkles with wonder.

Lover 4: My heart is yours. Like amethyst, it helps to cure addictions and bring peace.

Each hangs their heart on the tapestry. Then they bring out their wood slices with the bind-runes. Instead of hanging them up themselves, they hang them up all together.

Lovers (together): This is our vow to each other:
That we are bound together, but give each other freedom.
That we are solid together, yet able to grow and stretch.
That we live as one family, but are our own souls.
That we share our bodies, but they belong to each of us.
That we share our possessions, but respect each others' spaces.
That we have one love between us,
But we acknowledge that we are four different people,
Each with our own needs and desires and expectations,
And that this is as it should be.
This is our vow to each other:
That our love is stronger than the winds of change,
The heat of anger, the erosion of tears,
The chains of silence, and the ravages of time.
So mote it be!

Everyone echoed "So mote it be!" Then the rest of the folks present came forward, one at a time, and wove in their pieces of yarn and tied on their charms, explaining what wishes they symbolized for the happiness of this new relationship. Each offering was met with applause. Afterwards, the tapestry was ceremonially carried into their home, where it was hung on the wall in the heart of the house to be seen forever. The rite was over, and everyone feasted and partied.

Pluto

The Burning Ground

"Why is fire the symbol for truth? Because without truth, there is no light in the darkness, no warmth in the cold, and you wear out your teeth on rawness. And also, like fire, truth can destroy you, burn you to a crisp . . . but only if you haven't learned the secret of being the Phoenix."

—Jack Roe

The planet Pluto, astrologically, is the planet of transformation. That doesn't necessarily mean the slow evolution of the caterpillar into the butterfly, quietly done whilst the creature sleeps peacefully in a cocoon. More often, Pluto is about more painful transformations, done wide awake and with open eyes. Transits of Pluto can feel more like the painful labor of giving birth to a child than any quick shapeshifting. Pluto is the ruthless tide of Karma, insisting that you get on with whatever evolution your soul is supposed to be going through. If you refuse to take up that evolution actively, it might be forced upon you.

Polyamory is a volatile emotional practice. It is fraught with issues of trust, insecurity, jealousy, envy, territoriality, and misanthropy. It can bring up every painful issue from your previous life up until now, every wound that you thought you'd healed and every hot button that you thought you'd hidden. So far this book has mostly been concerned with the emotional comfort of the participants; a primer for keeping your poly relationships from flying apart. However, there comes a time in everyone's existence, sooner or later, when being comfortable becomes utterly beside the point. This time is often when the harsh, unforgiving energy of Pluto enters your life, although you may not recognize it at the time.

If it is done carefully, with honesty not only toward others but toward yourself, polyamory can be part of a vehicle for spiritual change and evolution. Let's give a non-polyamory example to start with: Jane has irrational fears and anxieties about car accidents, due to an accident that she was involved in as a child. With all her past lovers, she's waited anxiously and in torment by the phone whenever they were an hour late, imagining that they are wrecked on the road somewhere. When Joe starts dating her and discovers this fear, he offers to carry a cell phone at all times, so that when he's late Jane can call him and make sure that he's all right. This isn't a bad thing; in fact, it shows a great deal of consideration and compassion on Joe's part and can help build a lot of trust between them. Jane's reaction is likely to be positive—finally, someone who takes my anxieties seriously and cares enough to help lower my triggers!

The question is, however: How long is this going to go on? If Joe and Jane's relationship survives into old age, will he still be carrying a cell phone and getting occasional frantic calls from her until one of them dies or they are finally committed to the same nursing home? Again, this isn't necessarily a bad thing, but neither is it the end of the problem. While his consideration can alleviate a great deal of her anxieties, the other half of the equation is still hers: to work hard to overcome her anxieties, until ideally the cell phone is ultimately no longer needed.

This is the touchiest subject of all in discussions of polyamory. While all the negotiating and compromising and deciding who will do what for the emotional comfort of whom is all well and good, it should ideally be a cocoon in which each person grows into a more secure individual who no longer needs those compromises. Of course, this step is a difficult one and requires a lot of personal commitment to self-honesty on the parts of everyone involved. It rather depends on the values of the individuals involved, and values, like many other things, can change over the course of one's lifetime. Which is more important to you: emotional comfort or spiritual growth? You can't have both. It doesn't work that way.

I'll bring up another example, this one more personal and directly relevant. When the contract in the Saturn chapter was written, over a decade ago, I felt very strongly about having complete say over anyone that my primary partner touched, and I also felt that a serious, long-term, live-in secondary ought to grant me the same rights. Without that measure of control, I felt that I would simply be tormented by my territorial instincts to the point of great resentment and eventual breakup. Of course, as a responsible polyamorist, I was quite willing to grant them the same rights over me and my wandering genitalia, and I worked hard on seeing their prospective lovers as objectively as I could, rather than vetoing them for reasons of personal insecurity. This situation worked well for several years, as I simply wouldn't raise anyone who wasn't comfortable with this restriction past the level of fuckbuddy.

Then, within the last year or so, I got a secondary with whom I very quickly developed a strong, committed, loving relationship, and he moved in with us. My wife approved of him and even let him into our bed (fortunately we have an enormous antique bed and there's plenty of room), and all seemed well . . . except for one thing. He was a part-time sacred prostitute in service to the love goddesses, and several times a year he has vowed to serve in their temple as a priest/prostitute. During those times, although he may set limitations on activities, he cannot refuse anyone some appropriate form of sexual contact as long as they are respectful and treat the space and the service as a sacred gift.

Suffice it to say that there was a lot of drama over this obligation at first, as my control issues all asserted themselves at once, at the top of their lungs. The worst part was that, as a shaman, I am painfully aware that when the gods demand you serve them, you cannot refuse. To ask him to flout and reject his spiritual practices was unthinkable for me. In times past, I would simply have dismissed him as unsuitable, but there was so much love between us . . . certainly we could work something out?

Then, in the midst of this difficulty, another old lover came back into my life after a long absence in faraway parts. She and I had never been more than fuckbuddies and good friends, as distance and time were inhibiting factors, but I'd always welcomed her occasional visits. It turned out that she, too, had formally become a sacred prostitute for Baphomet, and she was getting ready to have the words "sacred slut" tattooed on her back in honor of that job. Unlike my lover, she would be "on duty" at all times that she was not actually doing something else; she has vowed to give freely of her body to anyone who asked her respectfully and wasn't underage or incompetent.

I'd never had any control agreement over her lovers, but it blew my mind that I suddenly found myself sleeping with two sacred prostitutes . . . and not as a client for either of them; in fact, my old friend said that I was someone she could go to for relief from her job. I like to think that there's no such thing as coincidence, just the gods trying to tell you something. When they stack up the clue-by-fours in that way, you have to squeeze your eyes tightly shut and plug your ears not to figure out what's going on. The Powers That Be were clearly saying, "Enough is enough. You've had your nice, safe relationships where you insulated yourself from your own triggers, and that should have given you the time and space and love and trust to be ready to face and deal with them. It's time now. You need to outgrow this blockage and be able to give those that you do love and trust the gift of free choice with no emotional strings attached."

I should make it clear that everyone's karmic timetable is different, and some people may not be required to face these sorts of lessons before the end of their lifetime, although I think that might almost guarantee that they'll be a major feature in the next one. Not everyone will have the gods come down, smack them, and say, "Now. It's time. Get over it. Grow, or else." Some might go for years allowed to be merely comfortable, especially if they're still working out the basic trust problem.

And some, of course, might be brave enough to do what I could not and deliberately work at all times toward a place of complete trust and generosity with those who have earned it, a place where compersion has completely replaced insecurity. It's a hard path but a worthy one, and it's the way in which polyamory can become a path for spiritual growth. Now, eleven years after crafting that initial contract of which we were so proud, I find myself looking at it and realizing that I am actively evolving toward no longer needing any controls over my lovers' choice of lover. Strangely enough, I don't feel resentful of them wanting to keep any control over my choices; this trust is mine alone, and I don't expect them to share it. After all, I know what it's like to be in that clinging, controlling space . . . how could I not? But I'm moving toward a point that I can just barely see in the distance, and when I reach that point, several of the lines in that contract will be irrelevant for me. I'll still insist on safe sex practices, as that's a matter of physical safety for my family, but that's all.

Of course, I didn't get even this far along that path without a lot of excruciating work. I spent many nights searching my soul, doing binding spells, meditating, and wrestling with my internal demons. I'd always done that periodically, but the difference was that now I couldn't afford to lose. If I lost the fight with my own territoriality, I'd lose my lover, and that would have been far worse. The Powers That Be know the right carrots to dangle, in the end. Eventually, I worked out a way to be reasonably at peace with my lovers' respective spiritual obligations, and I get a little further all the time. I realize that I could never be even this far down this path if I hadn't had that time of perfect safety, with all those rules and restrictions for padding and insulation while I banged up against my own spiked walls. They were necessary to teach me what real trust was. But now that I've learned that, I don't get to stay here. I have to get to the point where I don't need the training wheels for radical trust.

Radical trust is one of the ways in which polyamory can be used as a tool for spiritual improvement; another is radical honesty. This can best be defined as a situation existing between two or more people in which nothing is said in anything but the most blunt and honest way. In radical honesty, you not only do not hold back anything that you'd like to say to someone or that you think they ought to know, you don't soften or slant or put any spin on the way it comes out. Similarly, you expect no such verbal coddling from them.

We've often said that radical honesty has certain things in common with the practice of BDSM, and that many of the same rules apply. These are, in order of importance:

1. Like BDSM, radical honesty should only be practiced between two or more consenting adults who have all enthusiastically agreed to participate. It is never to be used on anyone who did not specifically consent to it, such as the checkout girl at the food mart, or your sniffling coworker, or your mother-in-law. This is because it may require you to dispense with courtesy, and courtesy is a very necessary ingredient in keeping the wheels of general non-intimate human interaction rolling. Without courtesy, there would be a lot more murders. Just as certain kinds of physical contact are inappropriate for someone who did not consent to a certain level of intimacy with you, radical honesty is similarly confined to intimate, consenting relationships.

2. Like BDSM, it can't be practiced by one person in the relationship on an unenthusiastic partner without hurt and resentment building up rather quickly. Both partners must not only be willing but think it's a great idea. If, after trying it, one partner decides that it's not their cup of tea, then it should be abandoned. It should go without saying that no one should try to coerce someone into the practice of radical honesty by playing on their feelings, morals, or guilt. If they're not up to it, they're not up to it, and implying that they're less evolved because of their reluctance will probably only create bad feelings. In addition, if two of three (or more) lovers agree to practice radical honesty and their other lover(s) does not, it should be restricted to the two of them. (This may put them into the rather odd practice of letting loose something blunt and straightforward to one lover and then turning their head and saying something designed to soften a blow to the other lover, but that's the only fair way to do it.)

3. This is because, also like BDSM, radical honesty hurts. If you can't take the blows and not take them personally, if you can't find a way to love and appreciate it even when you're reeling from an unpleasant truth or point of view, then you shouldn't be doing it. When you can hear your lover say that painful thing straight up, without a lot of disclaimering or softening to make sure that your feelings will be hurt as little as possible, when you can feel that pain hit home, and instead of being angry or resentful or victimized, say, "Thank you, I needed to hear that, and it will be good for me to think about," you're getting somewhere. When you can crave that pain, when you can say, "Please tell me what you think about my actions, and I'll value whatever you have to say," and mean it, you're getting somewhere. When that discomfort becomes a real signal that progress is being made, you're getting somewhere.

Polyamory, with its constant need for at least a basic level of honesty, can become a framework for a discipline of radical honesty that can contribute strongly to one's spiritual growth. It isn't that you can't do this sort of thing in a monogamous relationship—you certainly can—but in polyamory, that base level of honesty is a requirement, whereas monogamous relationships can go a lot longer while mired in a state of denial. Since you have to be honest anyway, being radically honest is a slightly smaller step away. It can often pay off in shorter and more productive processing sessions, once you've gotten used to it.

If not everyone in a multiple-person situation is comfortable with radical honesty, this may require a bit of mental gymnastics, especially in group discussions. Brenna in Wisconsin says, "I have a radical honesty agreement with one of my three lovers, but not the other two, and they are often appalled at some of the things we say to each other. They know that we wouldn't say those things to them— we are much gentler with them—but hearing the harsh stuff flung does kind of shatter their images of us, since it makes it clear that we're the sort of people who could, if allowed, say those things and maybe would prefer to communicate in that way. It's taken some delicate processing to work around."

Joshua in Massachusetts says of his commitment to radical honesty with his partner: "My commitment to radical honesty often means I wind up hurting my partner's feelings by saying things I know he doesn't want to hear, and he does the same to me. Between the two of us, we place a great deal of value on acting out of love and respect, but none on courtesy or protecting the other's feelings. We agreed from the outset that we weren't in this relationship in order to be comfortable, and oddly enough we find it easier to trust each other when civility is dispensed with entirely. On the other hand, my partner's wife expects a great deal of courtesy from the both of us, and I often feel I have to be careful not to hurt her feelings. I follow her advice on how not to offend her, even if it seems entirely alien to me."

Fire and Blood: A Special Kind of Love Spell

This isn't the kind of love charm that most people would ever dream of doing. It is only for the very brave, the ones who are ready to take that step onto the thorny path of growth. It can be used to ask the Love Goddess to bring you the kind of relationship specified, or it can be used to formally acknowledge to her that you are ready to transform your existing relationships in this way. Use it at your peril, and may it bring you fulfillment in the end.

On a red cloth—the color of passion and struggle—lay out a cup of bitter but nourishing herbal tea, a dish of salt water, a sterilized needle (or razor blade, or some small sharp thing that you are already skilled at handling), a red candle, and a feather to symbolize Ma'at, the goddess of justice . . . and your submission to your own karmic lessons.

Take the feather into your hand and say:

> O Great Lady of Justice,
>
> Balancer of the Scales,
>
> You who give us exactly what we deserve,
>
> I have learned to be fair in love,
>
> And to make sure that each has their share,
>
> And no one is wrongly used.
>
> Yet I find there is more to love
>
> Than merely blissful stasis,
>
> And there is more to justice than mere fairness.
>
> Show me the hard road, lady,
>
> The road that leads to greater rewards,
>
> And light the way with your razor-edged sword.

Light the candle and say:

> *O God of the Fire of Truth,*
>
> *I have learned to be honest with those that I love,*
>
> *And to speak truth even when it is painful,*
>
> *And it has kindled a warm hearthfire for me.*
>
> *But now I must learn to take that fire into my own hands,*
>
> *My own body, my own heart and mind,*
>
> *And turn that honesty on myself*
>
> *That has been honed sharp and keen by my loving.*
>
> *I ask that the love in my life be like your fire,*
>
> *Ruthless, purifying, burning away all that is false in me,*
>
> *All that pulls me from my true path,*
>
> *And I ask that you give me the endurance*
>
> *To endure the burning even in the midst of torment,*
>
> *And never let the torment sway my love.*

Take a sip of the salt water and say:

> *O Love Goddess who rose from the salty sea,*
>
> *Give me the gift of tears that fall*
>
> *Not in self-pity, but in honorable struggle*
>
> *With my own demons, and may those tears*
>
> *Be honored by the ones I love*
>
> *And may they have patience with my striving.*
>
> *Let me never be less than compassionate with their own battles,*
>
> *And may we move down this path together,*
>
> *Supporting each other with open eyes.*

May every tear that falls be a victory,

A single step further on the path of my destiny,

And may they number in the thousands,

As vast as the sea from which you rose,

That I may sail on it to my far horizons.

Drink the herbal tea and say:

O Love Goddess who is the beautiful peacock

And the vulture who feeds on rotting meat,

I am prepared to accept the bitterness

Of the strong medicine that I know I need,

For my wounds have festered long enough,

And the healing cannot wait for my fears.

I ask that the love in my life deal me what medicine

That you think is needed for my healing,

No matter how hard it is to choke down.

Only write the lessons large and clear,

That I may not be allowed to fool myself into blindness.

Take the sterile needle or razor blade and prick your finger. Let three drops of the blood fall into the candle flame and say:

O goddesses of love and death,

I am willing to bleed and weep

That the love in my life be cleansed

And transformed into a thing of clarity.

I am willing to bleed and work

That my practice of love

Reflect nothing but the integrity

I ask that it may help me develop.

I am willing to bleed and keep going,

Never ceasing in my love

So long as it pushes me into further growth

And not further stagnation.

For I have come to the end of what safety can offer me,

And its soft road did not stretch even halfway to the goal,

And so I must go on without it,

Through the path of thorns and stones.

I have had the safe love,

The comforting love,

The love that taught me how to trust,

And now I ask for the challenging love,

The love that will ride that trust hard,

And make it, and me as well,

Stronger for the ride, the road, and the real life.

Blow out the candle and sit silent for a time, contemplating the choice you have taken. Then get up and go to your lovers—or if you have none yet, go out and be with other people—and wait. The gods will send you what you request, sooner than you expect.

Appendix I

Polyamorous Astrology

Astrology is one of the best divinatory tools that anyone can have when it comes to relationships. Unlike other methods, it can give you a clear picture of the romantic, emotional, and practical needs of each person involved and compare them with each other. It can also highlight the areas where people are likely to rub up against each other and cause problems, giving you the chance to head off the really dangerous issues before they become devastating.

If you're not a reasonably experienced astrologer, my strong suggestion is to find someone who is. Ask them if they know how to create and interpret a multiple composite chart. Don't worry if you don't know what that means. If they don't know what it means, find someone else who does. If they do, bring them the birth data (or the astrological charts, if you have them) of all parties involved in the relationship, and ask for the following:

1. Basic chart interpretation of each chart for all poly members.

2. Comparison charts done between each member of the poly family, including those who are not having sex with each other. As we've noted, sometimes those relationships are crucial to the success of the entire situation. This basically means placing one chart on top of another and seeing how the two people's stuff interacts with each other.

3. A multiple composite chart for everyone involved. A composite chart is made by finding the midpoints of all the planets between two or more charts and creating a separate chart as if it were a person. That chart is the chart of the relationship itself. Many astrologers don't expect to have to do romantic relationship charts for more than two people at a time, so it's crucial to find one who knows how to do a composite for three or more people at a time.

4. Run transits to the composite chart, looking especially for periods of difficulty, argument, vagueness, or change. This can give you a near-future road map for potential trouble times.

This is a lot of information, and it may take your astrologer several sessions in order to get it all across to you in depth and detail. Make sure that all the information is taken down in a form that you can refer to later. If the astrologer generally does verbal explanations, bring a tape recorder and have it transferred to writing later. You will all want to be able to recheck it periodically and have a reasonable understanding of what it means.

If you know what comparison and composite charts are, and you'd like to do the interpretation yourself, one option is astrological software. According to the astrology geeks that I interviewed, the best software for multiple composite charts is Solar Fire.

If you are fairly experienced at astrology—and by this I mean that you understand the basics of planets, signs, houses, and aspects; can erect a basic chart; can compare two charts and come up with useful information; and can create a composite chart between two people—I'll just give you the information on doing a composite chart for multiple people. This technique was developed by Robert Hand and explained in his excellent book *Planets in Composite*, which I highly recommend for anyone doing composite charts for any number of people.

Start with the planets. In a composite chart for two people, you find the midpoint between each planet; that's the composite planet. The midpoint between two Suns is the composite Sun, and so forth. For multiple composites, it's a little trickier. We'll start with three people and then expand further.

So you're sitting there with your chart and that of your two lovers in your hands, and you want to know how it will work out with all three of you. Calculating it by hand involves a fair amount of calculation, but nothing more tricky than arithmetic. First, write down the degree and sign of each planet and convert it to the number of degrees from 0 Aries, using the following chart. For example, a Moon at 17 degrees Virgo is 167 degrees from 0 Aries (150 + 17). After doing this for all the planets and the ascendants, average each person's number for each planet and convert back to sign notation.

Aries	0
Taurus	30
Gemini	60
Cancer	90
Leo	120
Virgo	150
Libra	180
Scorpio	210
Sagittarius	240
Capricorn	270
Aquarius	300
Pisces .	330

I'll do an example—imagine three people in a relationship with their Suns at 23 Taurus, 4 Leo, and 19 Pisces. I would first convert each to degrees from 0 Aries and get 53, 124, and 349. The sum of these is 526 and divided by three I get 175 and change—175 degrees from 0 Aries is 25 Virgo, because 175 minus 150 (Virgo) is 25.

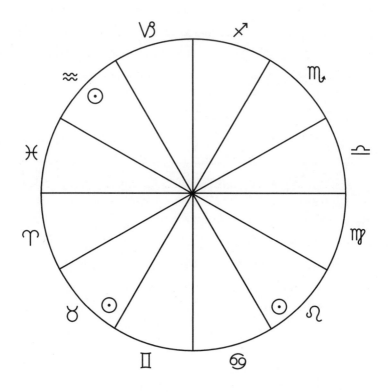

Here is the difficulty—In drawing up two-chart composites by hand, if the shortest arc between two planets spans 0 Aries, the composite planet generated by this method is actually directly opposed to the real composite planet and needs to be corrected. There is the same problem with composites between more than two charts, but the aspect isn't always opposition. One way to correct this problem is by recalculating the average based on 0 degrees Libra or some other sign. To check the calculation visually, mark the positions of each person's planet on a blank chart and verify that the composite planet falls within the shortest arc that includes all of the real planets. If it doesn't, for three people, move the composite planet to a position within the arc that is trine to the calculated composite. For four people, the correct composite position will be square or opposed the calculated one.

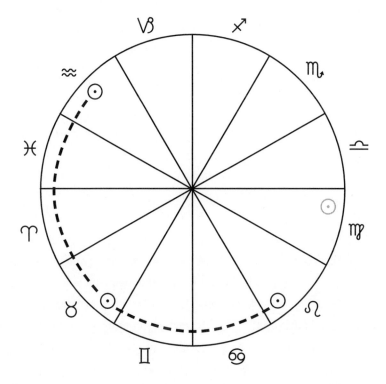

In our example, the calculated composite Sun at 25 Virgo falls out-side an arc drawn from 19 Pisces to 4 Leo, so it needs to be moved. Trine to 25 Virgo is 25 Taurus and 25 Capricorn. Only the composite Sun at 25 Taurus is within the shortest arc, so I would use that one. If I was doing a calculation and more than one of the possible compos-ite planets fell within the shortest arc, I could either use the one clos-est to the center or incorporate each of them in my interpretation.

Also, if you can't get your astrology program to draw up a com-posite for more than two people, but it can do a composite using weighted averages, you may be able to fool it into generating a mul-tiple-person composite. The thing to keep in mind is that if you find the midpoints between two people and then average that with a third person, the third person's placement gets twice the weight of each of the others. You can correct this by doing a weighted average of the first composite and the third person's chart, giving the composite two-thirds of the weight. Quads have it easier—draw up a composite of two of the four and a composite of the other two, then a composite of the two composites. You can extend this method to five or more, but it may be simpler to do the calculations by hand.

Continue to do the same for all the other planets and the ascendant. Remember that the composite ascendant is not the same as the composite cusp of the first house. To get this one (also called the "derived ascendant" as opposed to the "midpoint ascendant"), get an ephemeris and look up the ascendant and house cusps, using the composite planets, as if it were a single chart. The jury's still out as to which sort of ascendant better describes how the group will act outwardly; it is best to check both for potential information.

For longitude and latitude, use the place where the lovers all live. If they live in different cities, you might want to cast more than one chart, as the energy will vary somewhat depending on whether the "action" is happening in one place or the other. If you have two lovers who live together and a third who lives very far away, only visits occasionally, but corresponds often, use the living space of the two other lovers. The emotional action is likely to take place there, more often than not, as they respond to correspondence.

You might also want to have two-person composites for each specific relationship within your poly family to compare to the group composite. These will show how each of you act when you're alone together, as opposed to the will of the larger group. Take your time going over all of them; discuss them in depth. You can also run transits to a composite chart in order to find out the best time to take on a group project or when there will be especially hard times for your family.

Appendix II
Polyamorous Divination

The following divinatory layouts will work with Tarot, runes, lithomancy, or any other form of divination that involves laying out a series of objects. This is the most useful relationship reading that I've ever found, and it can be done for two people or more than two. This appendix demonstrates layouts for two or three individuals; you can add in more by expanding it the same way. The more people that you add in, the larger this reading is going to get, so make sure to clear a large space such as a bed or a large cloth laid on the floor.

Relationship Layout for Two

Lay the cards in the order specified by the diagram (page 242). The placement meanings are as follows:

1. Person A: their general attitude within the relationship.

2. Person B: their general attitude within the relationship.

3. How person B sees person A. May or may not reflect reality.

4. How person A sees person B. May or may not reflect reality.

5. How person B feels about person A.

6. How person A feels about person B.

7. Basis of the relationship: what sort of attitudes, activities, needs, or shared worldview it is founded on.

8. Biggest problem or barrier between the two people.

9. What needs to be done in order to solve this problem.

10. Probable future of the relationship at this time, unless something is done to change things.

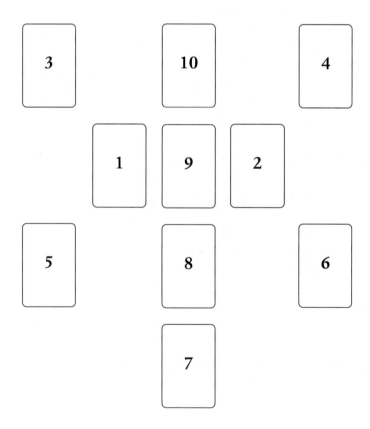

Relationship Layout for Three

1. Person A: their general attitude within the relationship.

2. Person B: their general attitude within the relationship.

3. Person C: their general attitude within the relationship.

4. How person B sees person A.

5. How person A sees person B.

6. How person C sees person B.

7. How person B sees person C.

8. How person A sees person C.

9. How person C sees person A.

10. How person B feels about person A.

11. How person A feels about person B.

12. How person C feels about person B.

13. How person B feels about person C.

14. How person A feels about person C.

15. How person C feels about person A.

16. Basis of the relationship between A and B.

17. Basis of the relationship between B and C.

9   A   4

1

15   10

27

24

21

18

25

22

19

16

14

8

3

C

13

7

11

5

2

B

12

9

17

20

23

26

18. Basis of the relationship between C and A.

19. Biggest problem or barrier between A and B.

20. Biggest problem or barrier between B and C.

21. Biggest problem or barrier between C and A.

22. Solution for A and B's problem.

23. Solution for B and C's problem.

24. Solution for C and A's problem.

25. Probable future of A and B's relationship.

26. Probable future of B and C's relationship.

27. Probable future of C and A's relationship.

As is obvious, one could keep expanding this reading from a triangle to a square, and from a square to a pentagon, and so forth. The problem is that with four people, you will have to do two readings with the positions swapped—A's section of the reading touches B and D, but not C. With a pentagon, the math is even more complicated, and someone with better math skills than myself should figure it out. Be sure to take notes and write down the readings, especially since there are so many placements with a larger group. You may want to refer to them later.

Appendix III

A Bouquet of Lovers:
Strategies for Responsible Open Relationships

by Morning Glory Zell-Ravenheart, 1990

(Note: More than a decade ago, Pagan priestess Morning Glory Zell-Ravenheart of the Church of All Worlds wrote this article and coined the term "polyamory." It doesn't seem appropriate for a book on Pagan polyamory to omit it, if only as a historic text . . . and to drive home that the word came out of our community to begin with, and it is unlikely ever to leave. We are blessed by a faith that values diversity as opposed to one that values stagnation. Never forget that it is actually a blessing.)

> *You want to know how it will be,*
> *Me and her, or you and me.*
> *You both sit there, your long hair flowing,*
> *Eyes alive, your mind still growing,*
> *Saying to me: What can we do,*
> *Now that we both love you?*
> *I love you too. I don't really see*
> *Why can't we go on as three?*
>
> —"TRIAD" BY DAVID CROSBY

et us begin with the a priori assumption that the reader is either currently practicing or firmly committed to the concept of open relationships as a conscious and loving lifestyle. If you are not in that category then this article will probably not be of interest to you. If you are full of curiosity about the potentials of open relationships, there are resources which deal with such soul-searching issues as jealousy management and theories about why the whole lifestyle is healthy and positive. Some of these resources will be given at the end and herein there will also be found considerable points of interest.

The goal of a responsible open relationship is to cultivate ongoing, long-term, complex relationships which are rooted in deep mutual friendships.

What elements enable an open relationship to be successful? Having been involved all my adult life in one or the other open marriages (the current primary being sixteen years long), I have seen a lot of ideas come and go and experimented with plans and rules to make these relationships work for everyone involved. There is as much variety in what different people require in a relationship as there are people involved in them. However, there are some sure-fire elements that must be present for the system to function at all, and there are other elements that are strongly recommended on the basis that they have a very good track record. Let us refer to them collectively as the "Rules of the Road."

Rules of the Road

The first two are essential. I have never met anyone who has had a serious and healthy open marriage that omitted these first two principles. They are:

Honesty and openness about the polyamorous lifestyle. Having multiple sexual relations while lying to your partners or trying to pretend that each one is the "one true love" is a very superficial and selfishly destructive way to live.

There are marriages in which one of the partners will state: "If you ever have an affair, I never want to find out about it." I suppose some folks take that as tacit permission the same way a child will connive when the parent tells them "Don't ever let me catch you doing such-and-so!" Without complete honesty, especially about sexual issues, the relationship is doomed. Some open relations have an agreement not to discuss the details of their satellite relations with their primary partner or vice versa, but there still must be the fundamental honesty and agreement that other relations do exist and are important to maintain.

The next principle mentioned is equally fundamental:

All partners involved in the multiple relations must fully and willingly embrace the basic commitment to a polyamorous lifestyle. A situation where one partner seeks polygamy and the other one insists upon monogamy or strongly politics for it will not work, for this is too much of a fundamental disagreement to allow the relationship to prosper. Sooner or later someone has got to give in and have it one way or the other. The truth is that people usually do have a strong preference.

> *Hogamus, higamus, men are polygamous*
>
> *Higamus, hogamus, women monogamous*

The only reason such mixed marriages have actually worked has been because there was an all-powerful church/state taboo enforced on options other than monogamy. In a patriarchy, men's deviation from that norm is ignored and women's is punished, often by death. The first recorded gender-specific law, in the ancient code of Urukagina from 2400 BCE, was directed against women who practiced polyandry, specifying that their teeth be bashed in with bricks. Now that the social codes are being challenged, even though the state maintains laws against legal plural marriage, both men and women are more free to explore alternative preferences, and relationships are conspicuously in a period of flux.

When I first met and fell in love with my present primary partner, I roused myself sufficiently from my bedazzled emotional state to say: "I love you, but I hope that we can somehow have an open relationship because I am not really suited to monogamy and would be very unhappy in a monogamous relationship." Fortunately, Otter was delighted to hear this as he had been too afraid of losing the new-found bliss to broach the subject first.

Many a relationship has foundered on the rock of Higamus-Hogamus. Nevertheless, the sooner it gets dealt with the better chance for the relationship to survive. It also means a quicker and kinder death to a romance if this basic agreement cannot be reached. Honesty and willing polyamorous commitment are the basic building blocks all partners must use to build a lasting open relationship.

Once over that hurdle, next comes a set of ground rules for conducting the relationships. Any relationship profits by ground rules, even a one-night stand. Nowadays, the state of sexuality being risky, such considerations are more than a politeness; they can be a lifesaver.

Never put energy into any secondary relationships when there is an active conflict within the primary. This has to be bedrock or the primary will eventually fold.

The difficulty with this rule is that if both partners are not equally committed to the openness of the relationship, it can be used as a gun in their disagreements. By deliberately picking a fight just before primary A goes to see a secondary sweetie, primary B can control her spouse and prevent him from ever having successful secondary relations. This behavior is fraught with dishonesty and secret monogamous agendas; if it is persistently indulged in, it is symptomatic of a fundamental problem with the basic principles.

If partner B plays this game with partner A's satellite assignations while continuing to pursue his own, B is an out-and-out hypocrite and needs to be called on his bullshit in no uncertain terms!

Nevertheless, this rule is the safety valve for sanity and preservation of primary relationships and should be followed with scrupulous integrity. It is a good idea for primary partners to have an agreed-upon set of signals or a formally stated phrase to politely request their primary to postpone or cancel the secondary assignation so that the energy can be put into the primary relationship for fence mending or bonding. This ritualized request can be structured so as to avoid loaded terminology and to decrease the negative emotional charge. Frivolous use of this signal is very destructive of it, as is refusal to participate in healing when access to the primary partner has been obtained.

Territorial jealousy has no place in a polyamorous agreement. However, situational jealousy can arise over issues in the relationship when one or more of the partners is feeling neglected. Obviously the best cure for neglect is to focus attention on what has been neglected; the relationship will prosper when all partners are feeling strong and positive about each other. From that strong and healthy center it becomes possible to extend the love to others.

Consult with the primary partner before becoming sexually involved with a new long-term secondary lover. The primary partner must approve of the new person and feel good about them and not feel threatened by the new relationship. Nothing can break up a relationship faster than bringing in a new person that is hostile or inconsiderate to the other primary partner. On the other hand, the most precious people in my life are the lovers that my primary partner has brought home to become our mutual life-long friends.

The check and balance on this rule is how often it is invoked by the same person. If it is used all the time by one person, this is patently unfair and is symptomatic of a problem or need that must be addressed. This can be tricky and once again, if honesty is not impeccably observed, the rule can be abused. If a man has a hard time relating to other men, for instance, he can use his alienation to pick apart every other lover his wife proposes on some ground or other, leaving her with no satellite relationship that is acceptable to him. The cure for this is for the person who has the problem relating to the same sex to seek a therapy group for people who want to overcome this alienation.

Different rules may be used to apply to one-night stands or other temporary love affairs. One-night stands are not necessarily frowned upon and can be a memorable experience, but some primaries choose to not allow any such brief flings as too risky, while others feel that such happenings add spice and are especially welcome during business trips or other enforced separations. The "ask first" rule may be suspended for the duration of the separation.

All new potential lovers are immediately told of any existing primary relationship so that they genuinely understand the primacy of that existing relationship. None of this hiding your wedding ring business! Satellite lovers have a right to know where they truly stand and must not have any false illusions or hidden agendas of their own. For instance, in a triadic relationship of two women and one man, there is occasionally a solitary satellite lover who wants to "cut that little filly right out of the herd." If satellite lovers are really seeking a monogamous relationship, then they will not be satisfied with the role of a long-term secondary relationship and it is better that they find this out before any damage is done to either side.

If a secondary becomes destructive to the primary partnership, one of the primary partners can ask the other to terminate the threatening secondary relationship. It is wise to limit this veto to the initial phase of secondary relationship formation. After a secondary relationship has existed over a year and a day, any difficulties with the partner's secondary must be worked out with everyone's cooperation. If you are not all friends by that time, then you are not conducting your relationships in a very cooperative and loving manner. When all is said and done, what we are creating is extended families based on the simple fact that lovers will come through for you more than friends will.

An additional complication can arise with the variable of alternate sexual preference. A bisexual woman I knew who was partnered to a man had to terminate a relationship with one of her female lovers because the secondary lover was a lesbian who objected to the primary relationship for political reasons. Another bisexual couple had a system whereby they were heterosexually monogamous and all their satellite relationships were with members of the same sex. This elegant solution underwent considerable stress and eventual alteration with the advent of AIDS.

Staying Healthy

Venereal diseases have been the thorn in the rose of erotic love for centuries, but recently the thorn has developed some fatal venom. If open relationships are to survive, we must develop an impeccable honesty that will brook no hiding behind false modesty or squeamishness. We must be able to have an unshakable faith in our primary partners and a very high level of trust with any secondary or other satellite relationships. This demands a tight-knit community of mutual trust among lovers who are friends. A recent study yielded some sobering statistics: over 80 percent of the men and women queried said they would lie to a potential sex partner both about whether they were married as well as whether they had herpes or other STDs. All it takes is one such liar and the results can be pathological to all. Nowadays, anyone who feels that total honesty is "just not romantic" is courting disaster, and anybody unfortunate enough to trust a person like this can drag a lot of innocent people down with their poor judgment.

In order to cope with this level of risk, a system has been evolving that we call the Condom Commitment. It works like this: you may have sex without condoms only with the other members of your

Condom Commitment Cadre. All members of the cadre must wear condoms with any outside lovers. The Condom Commitment begins with the primary relationship, where trust is absolute. Long-term secondary lovers can join by mutual consent of both primaries and any other secondaries that already belong. If a person slips up and has an unprotected fling then they must go through a lengthy quarantine period, be tested for all STDs, then be accepted back in by complete consensus of the other members of the cadre. The same drill applies if a condom breaks during intercourse with an outside lover.

Adherence to the Condom Commitment and to the other rules of the road may seem harsh and somewhat artificial at first, but they have evolved by way of floods of tears and many broken hearts. Alternative relationships can be filled with playful excitement, but it is not a game and people are not toys. The only way the system works is if everyone gets what they need. The rewards are so rich and wonderful that I personally can't imagine living any other way.

I feel that this whole polyamorous lifestyle is the avant-garde of the twenty-first century. Expanded families will become a pattern with wider acceptance as the monogamous nuclear family system breaks apart under the impact of serial divorces. In many ways, polyamorous extended relationships mimic the old multi-generational families before the Industrial Revolution, but they are better because the ties are voluntary and are, by necessity, rooted in honesty, fairness, friendship, and mutual interests. Eros is, after all, the primary force that binds the universe together; so we must be creative in the ways we use that force to evolve new and appropriate ways to solve our problems and to make each other and ourselves happy.

The magic words are still, after all: Perfect Love and Perfect Trust.

Appendix IV

Books for Polyamorous Pagans

Dreaming the Dark: Magic, Sex, and Power by Starhawk. Beacon Press, 1997. *Truth or Dare* by Starhawk. Beacon Press, 1989.

Although not specifically about polyamory, these books are excellent texts in group dynamics from a Pagan perspective. Starhawk's four-element discussion of the roles people play in groups, and the stages of relationships, should be read by any small group with a background in Neopagan symbolism. Polyamorous relationships, whether we like it or not, work less well with techniques used for couples and better with those used for small group dynamics. However, the political views in the books may put some people off. All I can say is that they don't really impinge on the useful group dynamics work; take what you can use and skip the rest, if you prefer.

Building a Magical Relationship: The Five Points of Love by Cynthia Jane Collins and Jane Raeburn. Citadel Trade, 2002.

This is a specifically Wiccan-oriented book on how to work on relationship problems, but the worldview expands without too much difficulty to other Pagan traditions and, to a certain extent, to other faiths as well. Good points are the really useful Tarot layouts and ritual exercises for lovers in crisis and the inclusion of polyamorous and same-sex relationships. This book is meant to be used by any sort of lovers in any arrangement; the sole exception might be lovers involved in a consensual power dynamic, but that's for a different book. Recommended for poly Pagans who are interested in using divination and ritual as relationship tools.

Handfasting and Wedding Rituals: Inviting Hera's Blessing by Raven Kaldera and Tannin Schwartzstein. Llewellyn, 2003.

Yeah, it's cheap and sleazy of me to include this one, but at the moment it's the best reference for nontraditional Pagan handfastings available. It contains plenty of gender-neutral rituals and wedding blessings, plus one of the poly rituals in this book. A good reference to give to the priest/ess whom you want to perform your poly commitment ceremony.

The Ethical Slut: A Guide to Infinite Sexual Possibilities by Dossie Easton and Catherine A. Liszt. Greenery Press, 1998.

The original ethical polyamory book, back when it was all still new. Still a great book, although largely geared for a young, hip, and somewhat-to-extremely queer audience. Those not part of any subculture may prefer one of the next two books.

Polyamory: The New Love Without Limits—Secrets of Sustainable Intimate Relationships by Dr. Deborah M. Anapol. Intinet Resource Center, 1997.

Entire chapter on jealousy, and lots of self-questions on preparing yourself for polyamorous relationships.

Loving More: The Polyfidelity Primer by Ryam Nearing. PEP Publishing, 1992. *The New Faithful: A Polyfidelity Primer* by Ryam Nearing. Polyfidelitous Educational, 1989.

Out of print but not very difficult to get through online used book places. Worth reading, especially if *The Ethical Slut* is too queer for you.

The Fifth Sacred Thing by Starhawk. Bantam Press, 1994.

Fiction novel by well-known Pagan author; although it's a bit too utopian and simplistic in places, it does have several well-rounded polyamorous Pagan characters who are out for more than just lots of good sex. Probably the best thing in it for poly Pagans is the beautiful love poem spoken by the character Madrone about seeing and appreciating all of one's lovers' other lovers, who shaped and changed them and made them what they are today. Worth copying down and putting on the wall.

BOOKS ON SOCIOLOGICAL AND SCIENTIFIC STUDIES OF POLYAMORY

Myth of Monogamy: Fidelity and Infidelity in Animals and People by David P. Barash, Ph.D. and Judith Eve Lipton, M.D. Owl Books, 2002.

Three in Love: Ménage à Trois from Ancient to Modern Times by Barbara and Michael Foster and Letha Hadady. Backinprint.com, 2000.

Anatomy of Love: A Natural History of Mating, Marriage, and Why We Stray by Helen Fisher. Ballantine Books, 1994.

BOOKS ON RELATIONSHIP SKILLS USEFUL
FOR POLYAMORY

Compersion: Meditations on Using Jealousy as a Path to Unconditional Love by Dr. Deborah Anapol. Self-published book is available at: http://www.lovewithoutlimits.com/books.html.

Love and Limerence by Dorothy Tennov. Scarborough House, 1999.

Love Between Equals: How Peer Marriage Really Works by Dr. Pepper Schwartz. Touchstone Books, 1995.

Intellectual Foreplay: Questions for Lovers and Lovers-to-Be by Eve Eschner Hogan and Steven Hogan. Hunter House, 2000.

Tell Me No Lies: How to Face the Truth and Build a Loving Marriage by Ellyn Bader. St. Martin's Press, 2001.

Radical Honesty: How to Transform Your Life By Telling the Truth by Brad Blanton. DTP, 1996.

Practicing Radical Honesty by Brad Blanton. Sparrowhawk Publications, 2000.

Organizations That Support Polyamory

Alternatives to Marriage Project (AtMP) is a national nonprofit organization advocating for equality and fairness for unmarried people, including people who choose not to marry, cannot marry, or live together before marriage. The founders, Dorian Solot and Marshall Miller, wrote *Unmarried to Each Other: The Essential Guide to Living Together As an Unmarried Couple* (Marlowe & Company, 2002). Their website, unmarried.org, has articles as well as an archive of personal accounts submitted by unmarried folks. Alternatives to Marriage Project can be reached at:

P.O. Box 991010, Boston, MA 02199
phone: (781) 793-0296
fax: (781) 394-6625
email: atmp@unmarried.org

Loving More is "a national organization and resource for people who wish to live outside traditional monogamy." They provide polyamory networking and education, and publish *Loving More Magazine* through Polyfidelitous Educational Productions (PEP).
Box 4358, Boulder, CO 80307
phone: (800) 424-9561
website: http://www.lovemore.com

The Institute for 21st Century Relationships is dedicated to promoting non-monogamous ways of relating as legitimate and responsible alternatives to "monolithic monogamy." They include unmarried heterosexual monogamy, same-sex relationships, swinging, polyamory, relationships with consental power-dynamics, and religiously motivated responsible polygamy. They host the annual Building Bridges conference in an effort to bring people from these communities together.
2419 Little Current Drive, Suite 1933, Herndon, VA 20171-4612
phone: (703) 561-8136
email: institute@lovethatworks.org
website: http://www.lovethatworks.org/

Pagan Groups That Support Polyamory

Church of All Worlds
The original poly-friendly Pagan church, mentioned elsewhere in the book.
website: http://www.caw.org

Four Quarters Farm

"An InterFaith Sanctuary of Earth Religion." Available for Pagan groups of any kind, including polyamorous ones, to rent the space for gatherings and retreats. Holds monthly new and full moon circles, as well as holidays and events, on their land in central Pennsylvania, most notably their annual raising of standing stones.

190 Walker Lane, Artemas, PA 17211

website: http://www.4QF.org

First Kingdom Church of Asphodel

Massachusetts-based Pagan church with commitment to sexual and gender diversity; strong percentage of polyamorous folk in congregation, as well as GLBT and low-income Pagans. Hosts "Tribeseekers," a yearly polyamory campout in July/August.

12 Simond Hill Rd., Hubbardston, MA 01452

website: http://www.cauldronfarm.com/asphodel

Spiritual Organizations That Support Polyamory

Sacred Space Institute

Founded by Dr. Deborah Anapol, author of *Love Without Limits* and cofounder of *Loving More Magazine*. Holds workshops, retreats, and seminars on sacred sexuality.

P.O. Box 4322, San Rafael, CA 94913

phone: (415) 507-1739

website: http://www.lovewithoutlimits.com

Unitarian Universalists for Polyamory Awareness

Check www.uupa.org for local chapters. Send email to UUPA @uupa.org or mail to UUPA, 16323 Linden Avenue North, Seattle, WA 98133. Offers UU-specific brochures and runs the UUPoly email list.

Internet Resources

The Internet changes daily, and I know how futile it is to assume that what I print here will still be around by the time this book comes off the press, much less six months later when you get it, but here goes anyway.

Polyamory Spiritual Network
Lists poly-focused and poly-friendly spiritual and religious groups, including Pagan and New Age spirituality.
website: http://www.polyamorysociety.org

For general polyamory discussion online, check the usenet newsgroup alt.polyamory and its associated website polyamory.org, as well as the polyamory sections of sexuality.org and altsex.org. Also, groups.yahoo.com lists many email discussion lists related to polyamory, many of them geographically specific.

If you're looking for counseling for your poly family:
Poly Friendly Professionals
website: http://polychromatic.com/pfp/

Appendix V

Pagan Festival Polyamory Etiquette, Or How to Not Screw Up in Front of the Entire Pagan Community

(Note: author Raven Kaldera originally wrote this as a flyer to distribute at Pagan festivals.)

O kay, so you're wandering around this Pagan festival, and you're running into people who practice polyamory. They seem to be openly romantically and physically involved with more than one person, and you don't know what to make of it. Maybe you're worried about how to deal with it. Maybe you're interested in trying it. Either way, this simple list of rules can help you to keep from making an idiot of yourself and from spreading disharmony around the event and the larger community.

If you have no interest in being poly, but you're just curious:

1. Polyamory takes many forms. Some folks who practice it have one primary emotional bond and have casual sex with other people. Some have several emotionally bonded partners, in various geometries and trajectories—triads, quads, chains, Vs, etc. Some have an exclusive group marriage—that's called polyfidelity. Some will refer to their partners as "primary," "secondary," or even "tertiary." Some don't use those terms. Regardless, saying "your partner" or "your partners" ought always to be considered polite.

2. Ethical polyamory is always practiced aboveboard, in the open, at least when it comes to people having romantic and sexual encounters. That includes partners of the "encountered one" as well. Polyfolk are not out to steal your husband or wife. An ethical poly person won't have a sexual encounter with your partner without not only your knowledge and permission, but your blessing.

3. No ethical polyamorous person will tell you that all Pagans ought to be poly, or that you're uptight if you're monogamous, or that you don't have the right to request that your partner be monogamous as well, if that was your prior agreement. If you get any of these reactions, you've just run into a jerk who is feeding you a line for their own sleazy reasons. Ignore them. They are not representative of polyamorous people as a whole.

4. If your heretofore-monogamous partner is looking at all the polyfolks and is pressuring you to let them sleep with that hot sexy bod over there, and you're not comfortable with it, hold your ground. Show your partner this flyer, including the last line of #2. Then, when you're back from the festival, arrange for couples' counseling. Obviously you both have some issues to work out together. However, it's better to work them out afterwards than to be screaming at each other on the car ride home.

5. If your lover goes off and boffs someone without your permission, you have the right to calmly confront them and the other guilty party and tell them that this is cheating, not polyamory. Note that I used the word "calmly." For the sake of the other festivalgoers, please try to keep it civil and reasonably quiet until you leave.

If you're thinking that you'd like to try out this polyamory thing, especially if it means that you get to sleep with new people during this festival:

1. If you're new to polyamory, and you're looking at all the happy poly people and you think you'd like to try this, wait. Don't jump in right away. Talk to people who have been polyamorous for some years. Find out about negotiations, boundaries, communication, and how to deal with upsetting emotions. It's best to hear these things from people who you don't intend to be sexual with. If you're not sure who to talk to, start with whoever's passing out these flyers. Ideally, they'll have a space at the bottom with the name and contact info of someone who's willing to explain polyamory to interested oncomers.

2. Keep in mind that festivals are sacred spaces and that they may feel like "time out of time and space out of space," where the ordinary rules of society are suspended for the moment. This does make some people feel as if the ordinary rules of their particular relationship ought to be suspended as well, whether or not their partner agrees with this idea. Keep in mind also that when you get together this many people who practice a sex-positive religion, there's going to be a lot of sexual energy floating around. This makes some people fall madly in love (or lust) with folks almost out of nowhere, and you can feel pretty foolish next week when the dust settles. Keep your head clear and a firm hold on your gonads, until you're sure things are safe.

3. If you aren't an experienced poly person—and by that I mean that you haven't been practicing polyamory (promiscuity does not count!) continuously and successfully for several years—

then you'll want to avoid anything that could even hint of deception and dishonesty. This means taking some rather draconian precautions, and maybe losing out of fun nookie with that gorgeous but shady hot bod over there, but please try to remember that there will always be more nookie eventually. We've seen some truly horrible public recriminations when people get overexcited and leap into bed without checking about that supposedly "understanding partner" first.

4. If someone says that of course they're polyamorous, but they don't want you to talk to or have any contact with their partner(s), be suspicious. They could be lying. It happens, a lot more than we like to admit. Either that or they're ashamed of you for some reason. Avoid the entanglement. You don't want to be someone's dirty little secret. If their partners are at the event, insist on discussing the possible liaison with them. Don't be a homewrecker.

5. If they aren't present at the event, ask to be allowed to call and talk to them, even if it's the middle of the night. Frankly, I'd rather be awakened at 3 A.M. than find out two days later about an encounter I wasn't apprised of. Again, they could be lying. I don't know how many times I've connected with someone who claimed that they had an "open relationship," but when I asked to be allowed to call and talk to their significant other, they turned pale, mumbled something, and ran away.

6. Some people have a "don't ask, don't tell" deal with their partners. While I'm not saying that this isn't a valid form of polyamory, I'd personally avoid doing it with them. The problem with this situation is that this is a small community, and sooner or later you will run into their lover. It's no fun to have someone giving you the fisheye across a workshop or ritual, won-

dering if you are the one that their sweetie boffed. It's also easier to hide cheating behind an alleged "don't ask, don't tell" policy. Remember, if you can't get their partner's blessing, it's probably not worth it.

7. Things to bring up at the negotiation: How much time will be allowed for you two to spend time together? Where will it happen? Is there some event that your interested party has to be at by a certain time, preferably with their primary partner? Will you be allowed to contact them later or to keep seeing them after the event? What are their safe sex rules? What sort of sexual activities are reserved for primaries only? (Some folks have some, others don't.) Most important: What actions on your part would make their partner(s) feel respected or disrespected?

8. Just because someone is polyamorous doesn't mean that they want to have sex with you or that they're necessarily looking to try anyone new. Don't assume that poly equals available.

9. Please make sure that the person you're interested in is over eighteen. Check ID. Check to make sure that it looks real—we know some teens who use fake IDs to get into bed with adults.

10. If you are drinking or doing other mind-altering substances, please sober up long enough to do your poly negotiations in an unaltered state. Refuse to negotiate with others who are not sober, regardless of whether they are your intended target or your target's loved ones.

11. Finally—and this ought to be obvious, but we'll include it anyway—use safe sex. Period. If you don't have latex, buy or borrow some. Don't be disrespectful of your own or others' bodies. You have no idea where people might have been, as recently as last night.

Also, a note to the already polyamorous folks who might be reading this flyer: We need to hold any and all Pagans who call themselves polyamorous to a high standard of honesty. If you run into someone who is using the poly label to get dishonest sex, spread the word about them. The grapevine is our best weapon. Warn newcomers. There will always be unscrupulous predators; the best thing that we can do is to warn their prey and spoil their game.

Have fun, be safe, and be careful. Blessed be!

☾ LLEWELLYN ORDERING INFORMATION

Order Online:
Visit our website at www.llewellyn.com, select your books, and order them on our secure server.

Order by Phone:
- Call toll-free within the U.S. at 1-877-NEW-WRLD (1-877-639-9753). Call toll-free within Canada at 1-866-NEW-WRLD (1-866-639-9753)
- We accept VISA, MasterCard, and American Express

Order by Mail:
Send the full price of your order (MN residents add 7% sales tax) in U.S. funds, plus postage & handling to:

> **Llewellyn Worldwide**
> **2143 Wooddale Drive, Dept. 0-7387-0762-7**
> **Woodbury, MN 55125-2989**

Postage & Handling:

Standard (U.S., Mexico, & Canada). If your order is:
- $49.99 and under, add $3.00
- $50.00 and over, FREE STANDARD SHIPPING

AK, HI, PR: $15.00 for one book plus $1.00 for each additional book.

International Orders (airmail only):
- $16.00 for one book plus $3.00 for each additional book

Orders are processed within 2 business days.
Please allow for normal shipping time. Postage and handling rates subject to change.

To Write to the Author

If you wish to contact the author or would like more information about this book, please write to the author in care of Llewellyn Worldwide and we will forward your request. Both the author and publisher appreciate hearing from you and learning of your enjoyment of this book and how it has helped you. Llewellyn Worldwide cannot guarantee that every letter written to the author can be answered, but all will be forwarded. Please write to:

Raven Kaldera
℅ Llewellyn Worldwide
2143 Wooddale Drive, Dept. 0-7387-0762-7
Woodbury, MN 55125-2989

Please enclose a self-addressed stamped envelope for reply,
or $1.00 to cover costs. If outside U.S.A., enclose
international postal reply coupon.

Many of Llewellyn's authors have websites with additional information and resources. For more information, please visit our website:

WWW.LLEWELLYN.COM